The Gift of Simplicity

Heart | Mind | Body | Soul

BROTHER VICTOR-ANTOINE D'AVILA-LATOURRETTE

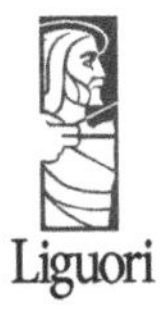

Liguori

Imprimi Potest:
Thomas D. Picton, CSsR
Provincial, Denver Province
The Redemptorists

Published by Liguori Publications
Liguori, Missouri
To order, call 800-325-9521.
Liguori.org

Cataloging-in-Publication Data is on files with the Library of Congress.

p ISBN: 978-0-7648-2746-4
e ISBN: 978-0-7648-6199-4

Additional copyright acknowledgments are on page 136.

Liguori Publications, a nonprofit corporation, is an apostolate of the Redemptorists. To learn more about the Redemptorists, visit Redemptorists.com.

Printed in the United States of America
20 19 18 17 16   6 5 4 3 2
First edition

CONTENTS

Introduction

But you are a chosen race, a royal priesthood, a holy nation, God's own people, in order that you may proclaim the mighty acts of him who called you out of darkness into his marvellous light.

1 PETER 2:9

All plenty which is not my God is poverty to me.

SAINT AUGUSTINE

When asked to write this book, I was rather hesitant. It is not easy or simple to write about embracing Gospel simplicity as a way of life. In writing about such a subtle reality as simplicity, one must avoid all that is superfluous and superficial, all that is intrinsically opposed to the beautiful reality of simplicity.

In trying to find the place of simplicity among those disciplines that foster the spiritual life, I discovered and became absolutely convinced of the all-encompassing role it plays in the concrete Christian experience of any true and sincere disciple of Christ. Simplicity opens up the path for assimilating and integrating into our daily lives all the teachings of Christ. The Holy Spirit, the Master who orchestrates and motivates our own personal spiritual lives, inspires us through simplicity to become more and more like Jesus each day. From the Holy Spirit we learn that to be found in Christ—or to be in Christ—we must be Christ-like. That is to say, we must become humble imitators of the Master. After all, Jesus clearly taught that the disciple is not greater than the Master. The best we can do to please him is to become more and more like him over time.

If anyone in history ever typified and exemplified simplicity itself, that someone was Jesus. He invited his disciples and all of his followers to join in the example of his own life. Jesus taught by word and deed how to live the lesson of Gospel simplicity with perfect trust in God and in the joy that belongs to God's children. The more we discover Jesus as a person, the more clearly we perceive the call to embrace simplicity in all its aspects as a way of life. From the Gospels, we get the straightforward understanding of how Jesus lived and breathed simplicity into every moment of his life.

During the silent moments of prayer and meditation on the Gospel texts, the Holy Spirit shows us, with a clarity that only he can conjure, that Jesus our Master honored the Father in heaven and served the brethren on earth with a transparent simplicity of life. Jesus made his earthly journey toward God, avoiding all worldly duplicity, traveling lightly, cultivating at all times that simplicity that unified his life and pointed all his earthly efforts to God alone. Ever since he left us that vivid example of simple living, it has become one of the signs by which we recognize a true follower of Christ.

For the sake of clarity and better comprehension of the role of simplicity in striving to live according to the Gospel, I divide this book into four parts:

1. Aspects of Simplicity
2. Simplicity and the Spiritual Life
3. Simplicity in Everyday Life
4. Simplicity and the Saints

Ultimately, these aspects and nuances of simplicity become integrated and unified in our own concrete spiritual life. The call to live out the Gospel daily is a radical one, and it embraces the paradox of having to embrace true simplicity while living in a very complex world. Thank God the Holy Spirit helps untangle the complexities of our time and guides us in the ways of inward simplicity.

The different chapters of this book, each a basic essay or reflection on a particular theme, show how the reality of simplicity weaves into every aspect of radical Gospel-living. The last essays in Part IV portray the integration of simplicity into the lives of the Mother of God and certain saints, especially those who spring from the monastic desert tradition. At all times, both in the Bible and in the monastic tradition, the desert exemplifies the place where radical simplicity is put into daily practice. Jesus invites his disciples to follow him into the desert, where simplicity is the daily bread of the disciple. In the process of discovering the transforming power of simplicity as an authentic pattern of Christian living, the disciple is given a taste of the Lord's promise: "Come to me.... For my yoke is easy, and my burden is light" (Matthew 11:28–30).

BROTHER VICTOR-ANTOINE
APRIL 20, 2008
FOURTH SUNDAY OF EASTER

PART ONE

Aspects of Simplicity

Simplicity of the Heart

Our hearts are made for You, O Lord,
and in You alone they can find rest.
SAINT AUGUSTINE

We rarely hear anyone these days speak about "simplicity of heart." In fact, it seems an almost farfetched notion, an archaic concept that is not applicable to our times when opposite values are exalted. Yet the concept is very alive in the Scriptures, particularly in the Gospels, where it is often connected with other virtues taught by Jesus, such as humility, poverty of spirit, single-mindedness, meekness, and even the gift of wisdom.

To gain insight into the importance the first Christians attached to simplicity, we must explore the Book of Acts: "Day by day, as they spent much time together in the temple, they broke bread at home and ate their food with glad and generous hearts, praising God and having the goodwill of all the people. And day by day the Lord added to their number those who were being saved" (Acts 2:46–47). We know from this account that those first Christians routinely embraced the gift and practice of simplicity of heart.

Today there is no doubt that they were impregnated with this gift of simplicity on that very first Pentecost by the infusion of the Holy Spirit in their lives. They chose to continue practicing and living the gift of simplicity as the Master had taught and lived it. They remembered the Lord's teaching when he said: "Blessed are the pure in heart..." (Matthew 5:8), which could have easily been translated: "Blessed are those of simple heart...." When Jesus said,

"Blessed are the pure of heart," he implied a much broader meaning for the word "pure." He suggested a wholesomeness, a single-minded orientation towards God and neighbor—an uncluttered heart, free to seek God's pleasure in all things. This simplicity of heart allows us to remain centered in God alone. For these people, not surprisingly, he promised: "…they shall see God."

The desert monks and nuns of Egypt, like the first Christians, had a profound intuition regarding the pivotal role "simplicity of heart" would play in their spiritual lives. They cultivated this interior attitude in many fashions, depending on their personalities, vocations, culture, and the formation they had received as disciples. Invariably, all of them understood the crucial necessity of keeping a single-minded heart in order to one day achieve the vision of God. They deeply treasured this *simplicitate cordis* that allowed them to remain humble, inwardly harmonious, and constantly in prayer as they sought to behold God's face. Abba Poemen, for instance, never stopped reminding his disciples of the unique role the heart played in their daily spiritual lives by saying: "Teach your heart to guard that which your tongue teaches."

Today we conceive of the heart as the seat of all human emotions. However, the prophets and the entire biblical tradition, including Jesus himself, considered the heart to be center of the human person, its very source of life. The heart is invited to love God above all things. The heart is inclined to obey or disobey God's commandments, for it is in the depths of the human heart that God inscribes his law and commandments. The heart is the very center of each human being; thus we learn that in each human heart, God wishes to establish his most intimate dwelling.

The desert monks emphasized among their disciples the uniqueness and special role of the heart in their spiritual lives. For them, the heart is the place where God reveals himself to us, where he relates and converses with each of us intimately. It is in the depths of our hearts that this relationship with God is established, grows, and achieves its purpose. As we welcome God's presence into the depths of our hearts, we are able to give ourselves to him wholly in love. With true simplicity of heart, we look at him and also sense his gaze upon us. We embrace and are embraced by him. The human heart, created by God, will recognize and accept that it is made for him alone.

It is our daily task as Christians to aim and seek this humble simplicity of heart. The Lord extends us his grace, and Christ is there to purify us of our sins and forgive our daily shortcomings. Through constant prayer and good works, we also make recourse to the Holy Spirit, begging him to descend into our hearts and make his permanent dwelling there. It is through the Holy Spirit, the author of all gifts, that the humble gift of simplicity shall be bestowed and implanted in our hearts. It is him, in his wisdom, who shall seal the gift deeply within us, creating in the depths of our hearts the living sign of his eternal presence.

Lord,
If you try my heart, if you visit me by night,
if you test me, you will find no wickedness in me;
my mouth does not transgress.
As for what others do, by the word of your lips
I have avoided the ways of the violent.
My steps have held fast to your paths;
my feet have not slipped.

PSALM 17:3–5

Simplicity of the Intellect

Open my eyes, so that I may behold
wondrous things out of your law.
PSALM 119:18

Throughout the many years of praying, studying, writing, and sacred reading, I have come to realize more and more that the priceless gift of simplicity lies in the power to transform our minds, hearts, and imagination. Simplicity, more than anything else, possesses the capacity to go beyond the very ordinary boundaries of our narrow minds, allowing us to discover that there lies ahead an entirely different world, a world where divine grace and the human experience interplay in perfect harmony. Simplicity of mind provides us with the intuition of how important it is to remain open to a universe where the peace of God and the freedom of all God's children can be experienced daily, where love and compassion are its daily bread, where acts of courage and sacrifice are undertaken not for selfish reasons but always in view of the common good, and where conflicts and tensions are overcome by dialogue and good will, not by violence or war.

Indeed, from our daily human experience we come to realize the complexities and difficulties that exist in the world around us. They are certainly manifold: we witness daily the inner conflicts between our bodies and our souls, the uneven tensions between the mind and our emotions, the disagreements between the individual and society, the rupture between humanity and the environment. Often we feel deeply threatened, impoverished, and conflicted by the weight of these tensions and the seeds of destruction sown all around us. As Christians, how do we confront these enormous conflicts and find a solution that conforms to our faith and values? It seems to me that the answer can only be found in the wisdom of the Gospel, in its fundamental message of simplicity, based on the authentic teachings of Jesus, who with his very life taught us how to live, how to train our minds and convert our hearts to conform to God's ways.

Inspired by the example and words from the Master, the Christian is encouraged to strive for the attitude of single-mindedness expressed in the Gospel, or what may plainly be called simplicity of the intellect. This intellectual simplicity exposes our minds to the clear light that comes from God, to the light of truth that we find in the words and message of Jesus. Filled with deep humility, we must freely acknowledge and accept the limitations of our own minds and readily renounce all our other intellectual presumptions and illusions.

Nothing is more deadly to the spiritual life than an attitude of vanity, arrogance, and pride, which we often see present in ourselves in subtle and uncanny ways. Once we have confronted our own stark reality, having renounced our sense of superiority and other self-interests, we may acknowledge and accept our limitations: we know and understand nothing.

We cannot go beyond a certain limit where our understanding reduces to *nihil*; our minds, enlightened with the gift of simplicity from the Holy Spirit, become capable of pursuing the clear path of truth. As we move along in this new path, we receive light from above to discover that truth itself is a Person, for the Lord tells us, "I am the way, and the truth..." (John 14:6). He prays to the Father for each of us to the Father that we may be rooted and consecrated in this very truth (see John 17:19). Grasping this truth, however, is far beyond the normal capacities of our limited minds. Nevertheless, Christ is there, present and ready to help us. Gently he guides us with his grace, directing all those who seek him with true simplicity of mind and humble purity of heart to the discovery of the fullness of truth found in him alone. Thus, in his infinite mercy, he grants us to walk the path to his kingdom where truth, light, and love flourish abundantly.

The spiritual connection between simplicity and the human mind is a unique one. Simplicity trains the mind to let go of reckless presumptions, speculations, and obsessions. It encourages the mind to remain centered on the one necessary thing, always fully open, honest in all its pursuits, consistent and frank in all its research and assessments. The simple mind is always loving and non-judgmental toward other human beings, discovering instead the wealth and fullness of life contained within each person, made as they are in the image and likeness of God. Simplicity always strives for utmost clarity, the sort of clarity and perspective that nourishes and enlightens our understanding. Finally, simplicity teaches our minds to empty themselves of all that is ugly and negative, choosing instead that which is beautiful, free, and positive. These qualities are contagious and convey to others the joy of following Jesus and the freedom and delight that comes with knowing ourselves to be God's children.

Lord God,
Behind the depths of our consciousness
lies the perduring limitations of the human mind.
All human life is immersed in complexity,
deeply buried under our rippled minds.
As our minds search for you,
may we encounter the supporting ocean
of your mercy and love.
Guide our steps in true simplicity,
that our small created minds
may one day transcend all human ignorance
and discover instead the riches of your wisdom.

BROTHER VICTOR-ANTOINE

Simplicity of Detachment

Be on your guard against all kinds of greed;
for one's life does not consist
in the abundance of possessions.

LUKE 12:15

The Desert Fathers and Mothers, our ancient mentors in the monastic life, always emphasized the importance of detachment for anyone who truly sought a spiritual life. They taught their disciples that letting go of the self, one's reputation, one's possessions, and one's achievements was very much a part of the essence of spiritual life. There was no compromise there!

When we first start to become serious about having a spiritual life, they tell us, we must also begin the process of learning to let go of things, allowing God to take over our lives completely. For beginners, this is quite a profound revelation. Slowly, we awaken to the realization that there is much we must let go of: the self we have known and cultivated all these years, with its firm opinions and expectations, the self we have projected to others, with its complexities and enduring reputation. We must gradually let go in order to become truly receptive to the gift of God's life in us and its continuing growth within. This is the moment when we find ourselves in much need of God's grace and intense personal prayer, the only tools that can help us overcome our fears and eventually open us wholeheartedly to the reality waiting ahead of us. Letting go is part and parcel of all authentic spiritual journeys.

In the deep intimacy of our hearts, each one of us knows which obstacles and possessions, including our personal preconceived notions of the spiritual life, we must eventually relinquish in order to awaken to the direct action of God in our lives. Inner simplicity helps greatly in the journey towards the spiritual transformation we seek. Simplicity encourages and shows us how to proceed and gradually let go of everything. It encourages us to leave our worries about the past, including our own sinfulness, aside. Simplicity, enlightened by faith, assures us that there can be gladness and joy in letting go of our concerns about the present and the future because our Father in heaven watches over every detail of our lives. Simplicity opens wide the doors for this "letting it go" to take place, allowing us to be fully present to the graces given to us at that precise moment. The process of detachment may seem to us at times severe and formidable to overcome, but inner simplicity assures us of the deep joys and profound freedom that are its rewards.

Letting it go, self-stripping, self-emptying, renunciation...They all seem such cold terms, such unappealing concepts! But the truth is that learning to live with the paradoxes taught to us by Jesus in the Gospels is a large part of being a Christian. The Lord often repeated to his disciples that in order to live they must first learn to die; in order to gain eternal life, they had to learn to lose it; in order to possess something, they must first let go of it. The great art of Christian living is embodied by learning to live with these paradoxes on the ordinary everyday path of the Christian, and we dare not escape them.

As Christians, we are mindful of the gratuitous gifts from God. Every day we pray, "Give us this day our daily bread," as we beg for what we need with true simplicity of heart. We also accept with utmost simplicity whatever God provides for those needs. Indeed, we find joy in not having anything of our own or in possessing much, so that we may ultimately receive all—everything—from God.

Our attitude of detachment means that we surrender the totality of our lives, in utter simplicity, to our Father in heaven; that we allow him to take total control over our lives and that ultimately we let him dispose of us as he wishes. We endure the self-emptying process, through an act of pure faith, that eventually we may find our emptiness filled by the fullness of God. This is the true nature of the simplicity of detachment and the inner freedom it grants us as its most precious fruit.

As we reflect on the nature of detachment, we realize that there is no concept or idea more countercultural or difficult to grasp in our world today. Modern culture and the clutter of our lives tend to revolt against a concept such as detachment. It seems so wrong to people of our times to cultivate an attitude which is just the opposite of greed, materialism, self-assertion, possessiveness, control, manipulation, and consumerism. These are the values that dominate our present culture and go unquestioned by our contemporaries. How amazing to see people easily become fascinated by TV marketing and advertising, which tends to enslave and imprison us with false promises rather than liberate us. We forget how fleeting, how finite, are the pleasures produced by earthly attachments. Indeed, these are real barriers for anyone considering a serious spiritual life.

Detachment doesn't seem to entice or even reach the level of consideration for most people, even by so-called "spiritual people." An old monk, whom a long time ago I queried about the role of detachment in the spiritual life, answered: "People of today do not recognize its necessity for leading a true spiritual life. They are not ready to give up things, including their own ideas. They lack the wisdom to see that learning to gradually let go of the self, of things, is the best preparation one can have for the ultimate 'letting go' that inescapably one day shall arrive to all of us, over which we have no control....Confronting death is never easy for anyone, but for those who surrender to God and gradually let go of themselves, it seems somehow easier to accept life's finality in a more peaceful manner." I often reflect on the words of this old monk, who, though no longer with us in this world, left us such simple statements of wisdom, similar to those of the ancient desert monks and nuns.

The simplicity of detachment opens our minds to new possibilities in the spiritual life, new horizons never explored before. It also frees us from the prison of self-centeredness and the chains of our earthly attachments. It overcomes our deepest fears, such as the ones created by our need to protect ourselves from our own pitfalls and mistakes, something almost totally impossible to accomplish. Simplicity of detachment inhibits these fears at their very core. It encourages each of us to let go of ourselves so that more and more we may allow God to take full possession of us. In doing that, we learn to walk in God's presence with joy and inner freedom, with a light heart, finally liberated from the countless tensions that come from the false assertion of the self and its supposed righteousness.

Lord, You are my lover—My all!
You are the safe object of my longing,
You are the flowing stream, my sun.
I am your tiny reflection,
Free my heart from earthly attachments
That it may continue to grow in that simplicity
That leads directly to your heart.

BASED ON THE WORDS OF MECHTILDE OF MAGDEBURG

Simplicity of Compassion

Come to me, all you that are weary and are carrying heavy burdens, and I will give you rest. Take my yoke upon you, and learn from me; for I am gentle and humble in heart, and you will find rest for your souls. For my yoke is easy, and my burden is light.

MATTHEW 11:28–30

As we seek to live our Christian lives more fully, guided by the Gospel as Saint Benedict counsels in his Rule, we try to grasp and understand better what it means to live the simplicity of compassion. In my view, our minds can only begin to decipher this truth by thoughtful attention to the words and examples of Jesus himself. As I ponder the Gospels, I come to one particular passage in the Gospel of Matthew that speaks vividly of the depths of Christ's compassion. I am always moved by this particular account, for it conveys in no uncertain words the deep sensitivity and loving compassion of the heart of the Master for his fellow human beings. The episode takes place on the shores of the lake of Galilee, where Jesus is addressing a large and hungry crowd. Saint Matthew relates: "Then Jesus called his disciples to him and said, 'I have compassion for the crowd, because they have been with me now for three days and have nothing to eat; and I do not want to send them away hungry, for they might faint on the way'" (Matthew 15:32–35). In this lovely Gospel passage, we first see Jesus looking at the physical ache of a hungry crowd and then reacting to their pain in the very depths of his own soul. It is a special moment where his human glance captures the reality of the moment and of the situation. Filled with divine compassion, he seeks to remedy the necessity of those around him. It is nearly impossible for our minds to grasp the power of that simple, direct glance. It is a glance filled with the power of love, and we know there is no greater power than that.

Jesus, the lover of mankind, immediately apprehends, with his penetrating eyes, the distress each individual in the multitude feels. With only the loaves and a few fish brought by the disciples, he surprises his own followers. With his typical openheartedness and compassion, he goes so far as to transform the laws of nature and perform a miracle, seeking relief for the people's pain.

This man-God, this "Lover of mankind" (as the Eastern liturgy likes to call him), is a compassionate radical, as radical as only God can be. His compassion has the power to use extraordinary means to change even the laws of nature! His infinite love would stop at nothing where human suffering is concerned. We see, therefore, through this particular example of Jesus, how the simplicity of his compassion personifies for us the infinite possibilities of living and expressing daily the reality of love in the very moment and place where we happen to be. (The Gospels are filled with episodes portraying Jesus' compassion again and again in so many and different cases!) The first Christians were characterized and identified by the love and compassion they expressed for one another, and this remains our challenge today, for this is what the simplicity of compassion is all about.

I must confess that I have great problems when certain political or religious figures, claiming a certain Christian background, identify themselves as compassionate conservatives. This, of course, is an oxymoron. To equate the concept of compassion (in the Christian sense) with the term "conservative," is a contradiction in itself. Jesus' compassion, which portrays the human face of God's own compassion, is shown precisely in its very radical attitude (as God himself is radical) as a compassion with no limitations, going beyond our human understanding. While the term "conservative" implies by its very nature certain constraints and demarcations, the opposite is true for the term "compassion." When understood, compassion in the context of the Gospels and based in the example of Jesus is a huge, positive force, a power that makes us go beyond ourselves as we try to act in complete empathy with another human being. The simplicity of compassion allows us to transcend our limitations; it frees us from our sins and ignorance and challenges us to follow Jesus' radical example of love. It opens our hearts to respond with infinite pity, as the Lord did, to the needs of all those around us: the poor and the afflicted, the sick and the condemned, the reviled and the persecuted, the blind and the lame, the adversary and the prisoner, the hideous and the obnoxious, the despised ones as well as the enemy, the small and the powerless, those who hurt and those in tears. We find many types of people along the way, and to each and all of them we must be the Good Samaritan and offer our help and complete empathy. We must envelope and protect them with the tender veil of our compassion and understanding. We must learn to love them as God himself does.

The simplicity of compassion opens our hearts to the realization that part and parcel of being disciples of Jesus means the willingness to carry each others' burdens. The Christian cannot remain indifferent to the pain and suffering of others—to the injustices and deprivations of God's children—all of them also our brothers and sisters. The Holy Spirit pours into our hearts the precious gift of awareness of the needs and sufferings of those next to us, God's sons and daughters dispersed around the world. As we ponder their basic needs, wherever they may be, we find that the same Holy Spirit empowers us to try to find solutions to alleviate their suffering and pain, to comfort them as Jesus would have done. This same Holy Spirit, the Spirit that proceeds from the Father, molds Christ's own attitude in us. He nurtures in us this infinite capacity for compassion, a true compassion after the heart of God that becomes in the eyes of the world a sign and witness of God's mysterious, boundless love.

Praise be to you, O God,
the compassionate and merciful one!
To you alone do we turn for help.
Guide us in the straight path,
the path of those upon whom you bestow your favor.

BROTHER VICTOR-ANTOINE

Simplicity of Humility

He has told you, O mortal, what is good;
and what does the Lord require of you
but to do justice, and to love kindness,
and to walk humbly with your God?
MICAH 6:8

Humility seems such an outmoded concept in a world that is constantly feeding on self-exaltation and self-glorification. In today's culture, the worship of God has been replaced by the worship of the self. Like a dark cloud, man's eternal temptation and pride often overshadow the entire human landscape, rendering our efforts futile as we try to pursue some manner of spiritual life.

According to biblical tradition, pride is the source of man's original alienation from God. Human pride, the fallacy that we know better than God, stands at the outset of original sin.

Times have evolved and changed since the time of Jesus and the prophets; unfortunately, certain aspects of human nature have not. I don't know what it is about us humans that makes contrasting ourselves against others for the sole purpose of promoting ourselves above them enjoyable. What a deceit! Human pride is so subtle at times that one is not always fully aware when surrendering heedlessly to it. Truly, pride, arrogance, and self-aggrandizement of any form are deadly for anyone pursuing some sort of spiritual life. In all spiritual traditions, Christian or not, pride is always assumed to be the hidden partner of the evil one, the true enemy of the soul.

Saint Benedict, in one of the early sections of his Rule, wrote an entire chapter dedicated to the teaching of humility. He saw it as fundamental to undertaking an honest monastic life. Saint Benedict proposes twelve steps for the monk as he climbs up the mountain of humility. In these twelve steps he brings to mind the Gospel story about the Pharisee and the Publican, the same story repeated to us yearly by the Church at the beginning of Lent. This Gospel story, found in Luke 18:9–14, reminds us that the temptation to pride is an all-powerful one, remaining with us until the day we die.

Once there was an ancient monk who often repeated to his younger disciples that "inner pride dies only fifteen minutes after our own death." In his wisdom, the old monk knew that the battle to overcome pride was fierce, a battle that needed to be fought in the depths of our own souls until the very end. The old monk recommended one weapon to overcome this evil, the same weapon shown by the Lord in the Gospel story: prayer. The particular prayer he recommended was that of Publican: "God, be merciful to me, a sinner." Only through the continual recitation, day and night, of this short and simple prayer, said the monk, could true simplicity of humility be achieved and the evil of pride overcome.

Saint Benedict, deeply rooted in the tradition of the Desert Fathers and Mothers and having also learned from his own experience, had the incomparable intuition that the achievement of humility was essential to the monk who sought to live in close communion with God. The Holy Spirit, through the grace and simplicity of humility, provides the monk with the capacity to look into himself in honest self-appraisal, allowing him to glance at exactly where he stands in his spiritual journey. The simplicity of humility gives us the courage to look at ourselves and see in reality who we really are: slaves of our passions, sins, and vices; of our prejudices and intolerances; of a manipulative culture that exalts the self and prefers worldly honors; and slaves of the image we have created of ourselves: an idealized and false self which we like to portray to others for their admiration. Nothing is more difficult and more painful than to look at ourselves as we really are and accept it as such. It takes a great deal of courage, as well as God's grace and a deep and simple humility, to be able to do so.

Simplicity and humility are inseparably linked to each other. Like identical twins, one doesn't exist without the other. Simplicity opens the path to humility and provides us the deep desire to imitate Jesus, who was "compassionate and humble of heart." The path to humility is not easy, though. Like all things human, it is fragile and filled with pitfalls. During difficult and trying moments, simplicity comes to our rescue and in its own subtle and unambiguous way reminds us of the words of the Master who clearly taught us to position ourselves in "the last place" in all situations. In the words of Charles de Foucauld, "*Cette chere derniere place*" ("This is our dear last place"). Simplicity welcomes God's grace into our hearts, stirring them with the type of humility that makes us recognize and accept our deep woundedness, pointing out to us how deeply we need God's loving mercy. The simplicity of humility frees us from constantly investigating ourselves, from looking at our misery and shortcomings. Instead, it points our eyes to the loving glance of Jesus, to that glance full of mercy and compassion which can alone provide us complete forgiveness.

Jesus loved the humble of heart. Again and again he showed his preference for them in the Gospels. They captivated his heart regardless of if they were saints or sinners. He found himself most at home in their company. This is not difficult to understand, for there is an enchanting quality about those who possess the simplicity of true humility. In their quiet humbleness, these individuals tend to be transparent, poised, dignified, single-minded, and totally free of the self-centeredness that is so intolerable in God's eyes. The heart of the humble one is always enveloped in the total consciousness of God's gratuitous love. He or she never attributes anything good to themselves. They gladly sing with the Psalmist: "Not to us, O Lord, not to us, but to your name give glory" (Psalm 115). Like Our Lady, the perfect model for those seeking the simplicity of humility, they never cease to marvel at the great things the Lord has done for them. In this they find their true purpose, their true self, and the unique gift of peace granted to those who seek the Lord with simplicity and humility of heart.

> *"My soul magnifies the Lord,*
> *and my spirit rejoices in God my Saviour,*
> *for he has looked with favour on the lowliness of his servant.*
> *Surely, from now on all generations will call me blessed;*
> *for the Mighty One has done great things for me,*
> *and holy is his name."*
>
> LUKE 1:46–49

Simplicity and Silence

When the Lamb opened the seventh seal,
there was silence in heaven...

REVELATION 8:1

In an age such as ours, full of feverish consumerism, instant communication, loud music and noisy TV, it is quite a challenge to begin speaking about the reality of silence. Occasionally I am asked to give a talk to a group of people, either young students or adults. I often notice a visible expression of skepticism on their faces when I mention or stress the importance of silence in daily monastic life. The value and appreciation of silence in today's culture has dwindled. People consider silence sterile, and it has become unpopular. The wisdom contained in the practice and love of silence has been abandoned for the false values that are the product of present day culture: noisy and chaotic living, hullabaloo, hurried and frantic behavior, loud entertainment, and endless activities. The inner spiritual world that urges and appreciates the daily necessity for silence goes in one direction, and the world of today's culture goes in the opposite. Today, belief in the truth of silence is not only disregarded and underestimated, it is considered plainly outmoded.

In contrast to the frenzy of the world and its negative view of silence, Saint Benedict and the whole monastic tradition present us with the intrinsic value of silence as a prerequisite for wholeness. Silence, in its bare and stark simplicity, provides us with the quiet space and the inner energies needed to devote our full attention to God. There can't be much of a spiritual life without silence, the

Desert Fathers would tell us. When a new beginner arrived in the desert, one of the old spiritual fathers or mothers would quietly invite the novice to "enter into the sacred silence." One lovely anecdote tells of a dialogue that took place in a monastic desert, revealing much about the meaning and importance of silence. The story, a bit paraphrased, goes like this:

> "Would you teach me silence?" the novice asked.
>
> "Ah!" the old monk said. "Is it the sacred silence that you wish to learn and abide in?"
>
> "Yes, the sacred silence," the novice replied.
>
> "Well, where do you think it can be found?" the old monk asked.
>
> "Deep within me, I believe. If only I could go deep within, I'm sure I'd escape the weight of a noisy world at last. But this is hard to do. Will you help me, dear Father, to accomplish this?" The novice knew the old monk would. He could feel the his concern and the silence of his spirit.
>
> "Well, I've been there," the monk answered. "I have spent years going deeply into the silence. But one day Christ came—maybe it was my imagination—and said to me in all simplicity, 'Come, follow me.' Then suddenly I went out of myself, and I've never gone back."
>
> Stunned at his revelation, the novice asked, "But what about the silence?"
>
> The old monk replied, "I have found the sacred silence, and in it, I discovered that all the noise was inside of me."

For the young monk, the practice of silence provided him with the means to better understand himself: it was an end in itself. For the wise old monk, however, silence was a form of apprenticeship, a tool to discover a deeper reality: the fact that daily living is an art, and in this daily living, we are called to ascertain God's loving presence. Nevertheless, for both master and disciple, silence provided the nurturing environment, the required steadiness, to continue the inner search freely, happily, and in whatever fashion the Lord would lead them. The simplicity of silence was the initial act by which both monks, obviously at very different times in their spiritual development, initiated their inner journey. By the very real experience of "entering into the simplicity of silence," they were both able to savor the joys of divine intimacy.

During these very intense and silent moments of divine union, the light of God, the Holy Spirit, deciphered for them the meaning of Christ's words in the Gospels. They intuitively understood what the invitation to follow him entailed. Thus, the silence itself became a revelation, the clear voice of God in the depths of their own hearts.

In my limited experience, I have come to realize that the necessity for silence does not apply only to monks and nuns in monasteries and hermitages: it applies to everyone. Everyone needs to rediscover some silent, quiet space within himself or herself just to maintain basic sanity. The simplicity of silence creates this inner space within us, a space where the integration of our scattered powers becomes possible.

In this space, we cultivate both exterior and interior silence that fosters and builds up the inner unity of our beings. Silence creates that wide open space within, where guided by the Holy Spirit, we can come to the knowledge and experience of the living God and where we can better apprehend the mystery of his infinite love for each of us. Silence purifies our vision, cleanses our hearts, and strengthens and deepens our prayer. The simplicity of silence brings light and clarity to our minds; it grants peace, tranquility, and perseverance as we toil daily. Silence is the inner source of strength, harmony, and stability in our daily endeavors. It provides us with the groundedness we need, keeping us centered, reminding us always of what the Gospels calls the *unum neccesarium* (see Luke 10:42), that is, the only one thing that is necessary.

The masters of all different spiritual traditions always regarded silence as part and parcel of the inner life of the person. Silence is an organically unfolding reality, a most precious gift that enhances our capacity for knowledge, for repentance, for awareness, for prayer, and for wisdom. Silence expands our minds, opening them to new choices and possibilities. It empowers our hearts to humbly submit to the action of divine grace within us. It nurtures our capacity to hold a constant dialogue with the divine guest inhabiting our innermost existence. A spiritual writer once expressed well his appreciation for this type of silence:

> *The love of silence leads to that unique silence, the essence and substance of divine Love.*
> *Silence is the mystery of the world to come,*
> *Speech is the organ of this present world...*
> *Every man who delights in a multitude of words,*
> *Even if he says admirable things, is empty within.*
> *Silence, however, will illuminate you in God*
> *And deliver you from the phantoms of ignorance.*
> *Silence will unite you to God himself.*
>
> SAINT ISAAC THE SYRIAN

Simplicity and Non-judging

"Do not judge, so that you may not be judged."
MATTHEW 7:1

Christian simplicity contains a certain freedom, a simplicity that is deeply rooted in the Gospels. It is the freedom imparted by grace, the freedom of someone who lives entirely by God's gratuitous gift and henceforth has no need to attribute anything to his or herself, for he or she no longer makes any claims upon themselves except their own sinfulness. Christian simplicity enlightens and clarifies Christ's teachings. It gives meaning to every event or encounter in our lives and makes us see all things anew, in the radiant light of God's Holy Spirit. We begin to look at others kindly, with compassion and with deep charity, refusing all along to pass any negative judgment on them.

Many may ask what evangelical simplicity has to do with the Lord's injunction not to judge others. On the surface, these two concepts appear to have little to nothing in common. Yet we know that in the scheme of things, in God's mysterious plan, resides always a certain connection, a confluence, and that all things in the Gospel are interrelated. The Lord taught us, "'Do not judge, so that you may not be judged'" (Matthew 7:1). He also said that " The eye is the lamp of the body. So, if your eye is healthy, your whole body will be full of light; but if your eye is unhealthy, your whole body will be full of darkness. If then the light in you is darkness, how great is the darkness!" (Matthew 6:22–23). The single "eye" of the Gospel and simplicity of heart are one and the same reality.

In our desire to please God, we take seriously the commandment to love others and not to judge them.

Jesus, throughout the many episodes in the Gospel, gave us a perfect example of this and continually invited and challenged us to live by the commandment to love. He repeated to his disciples: "'By this everyone will know that you are my disciples, if you have love for one another'" (John 13:35). Jesus makes it poignantly clear that love is the origin, the source, the only purpose and reason for all Christian life. One of the forms of true love, the type of Christian love that distinguishes itself from others, contains and comprises the refusal to judge our brother or sister.

Our hearts open in simplicity to the fullness of God's love and bring us nearer to the heart of God. We begin to understand that the substance of true love is loving others as God loves them.

One of the most difficult Gospel teachings to put into practice is exercising this non-judgmental attitude toward any individual. Abiding by this mental attitude and practice is painfully difficult, almost as painful as the command to love our enemies. Sometimes, this may seem to us nearly impossible to achieve. Too often we judge others in an instant, even without fully realizing what we are doing. Our human minds have become so accustomed to acting this way that we do so automatically, unable to perceive our own judging. Yet, as Christians, we are reminded by the sacred Scriptures that judgment belongs to God alone. The early Christians, just as much as any of us, struggled to put this Gospel teaching into practice. It wasn't easier for them then, just as it is not easy for us now. The desert monks and nuns were not foolish when they placed a great deal of emphasis on the practice of not judging others. They knew from experience that it was impossible to live in a communion of love with God while continuing to pass judgment on their neighbors. They were deeply aware of the subtle temptation to pride contained within a judgmental attitude. For implicit in the act of passing judgment lies the assertion of our own superiority over the person whom we judge, making the claim that we are better than he or she. This attitude, so similar to that of the Pharisee in the Gospels, was among those Jesus found most reprehensible, most repugnant.

To overcome our judgmental attitudes, we need to retrain our minds and hearts in the school of the Gospel. In all simplicity, and with purity of heart, we must embrace the sort of asceticism that Jesus practiced and indicated for all his disciples. Learning to acquire a non-judgmental attitude is an integral part of the Christian ascesis demanded by the Gospel. Without any ambiguity, the Lord categorically asserted that our personal conception of others merits no value. He also unconditionally interdicted us, no matter what the circumstances, from passing judgment on others. Christ, knowing so well our human weaknesses, also knew how prone we are to exalt ourselves by often exaggerating and criticizing the faults of others. The Lord, always clear and to the point in his teachings, told his disciples in very precise words: "'For with the judgement you make you will be judged, and the measure you give will be the measure you get. Why do you see the speck in your neighbour's eye, but do not notice the log in your own eye?...You hypocrite, first take the log out of your own eye, and then you will see clearly to take the speck out of your neighbour's eye'" (Matthew 7:2–5). Obviously, this is not an easy teaching to put into practice.

Following our Lord's counsel on this topic creates a variety of conflicts within us due to our opposing sensibilities. On the one hand, pressing forward decisively with our spiritual life implies that we must endure the pains of this self-dying process, of this emptying of our judgmental minds. We must learn and accept daily to be crucified with Christ. Therefore, with deep humility and simplicity of spirit, we must face and accept our mind's limitations, its false tendencies, and pray to the Holy Spirit for the true regeneration of all our faculties, including our faculty to judge others. As we pray and act to liberate ourselves from all these obstacles within, we may suddenly discover God's loving hand leading us freely to the place of perfect stillness, where our wearied souls, having overcome themselves, may find true repose in God alone. So great is his mercy, so great is his love for each of us! *Quonian in aeternum misericordia ejus!*

O Lord and Master of my life,
take away from me the attitude of laziness, meddling,
ambition and vain talk.
Grant me instead an attitude of prudence, humility,
patience and love.
Yes, my Lord and King,
grant me to see my own sinfulness and
not to judge my brethren.
For You alone are holy unto ages of ages. Amen.

SAINT EPHREM'S LENTEN PRAYER

Simplicity and Gratitude

I will give thanks to you, O Lord, among the peoples;
I will sing praises to you among the nations.
For your steadfast love is as high as the heavens;
your faithfulness extends to the clouds.

PSALM 57:9–10

As in all things spiritual, simplicity and gratitude are always related. True simplicity brings great joy, and there is also great joy in gratitude, in living each day with a gentle attitude of simple, deep thankfulness to God for the gifts he bestows on us daily. These precious gifts make us deeply aware of God's infinite goodness, of his all-encompassing providence for us, and also of the total gratuity of his gifts. What have we done to deserve such love, such care, such attentiveness from a loving Father? The awareness of having received so much from God evokes a natural response: simple, deep, and total gratitude for the gratuity of his gifts, the wonders of his love, and the unique and tender manner with which he provides for our daily needs.

Every new day, every event, every thought, every relationship in our lives is a gift from above, a blessing from the Almighty. As this knowledge grows deeper and stronger in us each day, so should the wholehearted expression of gratitude in our daily prayer. Inner simplicity encourages us to keep silence within ourselves and lets this sense of gratitude to God become a permanent aspect of our prayer. During those intimate moments of communion with God, a distinct realization grows in us: in order to live by the gifts received from God, we must first learn to leave the choice of those gifts to him alone.

The Psalms, as prayer, are filled with sentiments and attitudes of gratitude towards God. The people of Israel were very conscious of the Lord's benefits and of his protection over them in their everyday lives. Again and again, they deliberately expressed their gratitude to the Almighty through the simplicity and depth of the psalms they prayed. We often find passages such as the one in Psalm 29 filled with utterances of gratefulness and thanksgiving:

Sing praises to the Lord, O you his faithful ones,
and give thanks to his holy name.
For his anger is but for a moment;
his favour is for a lifetime.

PSALM 30:4–5

As we make the Psalms of David an integral part of our prayer, our inner beings become more and more attuned to the all important role of gratitude in our daily lives. Gratitude is an inner attitude deeply rooted in the Scriptures and an integral part of all true prayer.

Just as much as the Psalms, the letters of Saint Paul are impregnated with teachings about gratitude. Saint Paul often tells us "to give thanks in all things," or to "abound in gratitude," or "sing psalms and hymns and spiritual songs among yourselves, singing and making melody to the Lord in your hearts, giving thanks to God the Father at all times and for everything in the name of our Lord Jesus Christ" (Ephesians 5:19–20). By acknowledging all that God's grace has accomplished in and for us, from the beginning of the world through our own individual existences, we can achieve this constant attitude of gratitude in prayer. Thus, attuned to this special grace at work in us, we turn to the Lord during prayer with a disposition of profound simplicity and gratitude. God shall take charge of our lives as we, in all simplicity, gratitude and faith, submit ourselves obediently and wholly to his continuing work in us.

Simplicity also shows us that this attitude of inner gratitude has certain implications: we must learn to live, at all times, by absolute faith and trust in God's providence. It is not enough to say: "Thank you, thank you, Lord": we must also learn to accept everything that comes from God's hands, both joy and pain. We readily accept joy; however, when we face suffering, we often choose to escape, though they both figure into God's ultimate plans for us. Living by faith and gratitude implies a humble submission to God's will in all things and throughout all events in life. We must not only wait receptively for his designs to be accomplished in us, but we must actively cooperate that they may be so. In this submission we shall feel tranquil and free, overflowing with gratitude as we rejoice in and accept God's pleasure and will for every detail of our lives. Our joy shall then be complete, for knowing that we are the object of God's loving kindness, his tender mercy for us, shall give us a taste of the eternal bliss we await in paradise.

Indeed, the concept and reality of gratitude plays a unique role in our spiritual lives. In the Gospels, Jesus encourages his followers to show gratitude always, going as far as to reproach the lack of it among certain ones. Jesus instructs the ten lepers, according to Saint Luke's Gospel, to show themselves to the priests, and on their way, they are healed. When only one of the lepers returns "praising God with a loud voice" and falls at Jesus feet to thank him, Jesus pointedly asks about those who did not return. To this one, a foreigner, Jesus commands, "Get up and go on your way; your faith has made you well" (Luke 17:15, 19).

Every day, we have many opportunities to put our faith into practice with grateful hearts. Jesus, the perfect image of his Father, wishes to transform each of us into his own image. He can only do this to the extent that we cultivate his teachings, try to imitate him in all things, and finally grasp the hem of his garments and hold onto him until the end.

From this particular Gospel episode, as well as from other Scripture passages in the New Testament, we learn that the Christian, perfected in simplicity and entirely enveloped in gratitude, is someone in whom God's grace abides naturally and spontaneously, even imperceptibly. That person need not be concerned any longer with how he or she shall go about continually expressing these sentiments of praise and gratitude. The presence of God already permeates their entire being. It is the Holy Spirit himself who prays within them and renders thanksgiving to God in ways and terms that cannot be described.

O Lord and Master,
We live by the utter generosity of your gifts.
In deep silence, we come to know how much
everything in us is the work of your grace.
In utter simplicity and with deep gratitude
we ask you, Lord, to take our lives into your hands
and to dispose of us as you wish.

BROTHER VICTOR-ANTOINE

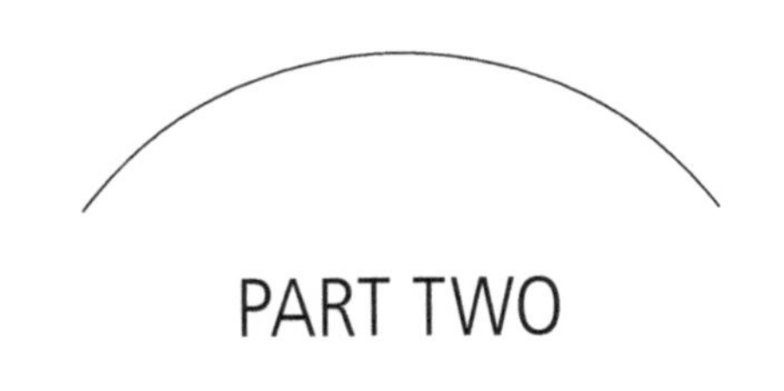

PART TWO

Simplicity and the Spiritual Life

Simplicity and the Desire for God

The whole life of a fervent Christian is a holy desire.
SAINT AUGUSTINE

One of the reasons I never tire of feasting on the early Church writings, either by the Fathers of the Church both Eastern and Western or the early monastic Fathers and Mothers, is the purity, straightforwardness, and simplicity of their teachings, rooted in the Gospels. Like Christ the Master, they don't mince words. On the contrary, they economize their words to go directly to what is essential.

This is precisely the gift of Christian simplicity, which refuses to waste time and energy dealing with the superfluous. Simplicity always leads us straight to the heart of the matter. Simplicity emphasizes that to cultivate the inner life, the life of continual prayer, we must first try to cultivate a well-ordered, well-directed Christian life, where the counsels taught in the Gospel flourish and blossom as in a beautiful garden. Through this blessed simplicity of spirit, we open ourselves totally to the Holy Spirit's inner workings, allowing him to bring order into our otherwise chaotic interior existence. It is the Holy Spirit who brings our scattered powers under control, forming a harmonious unity, opening the path to consolidate and solidify our sole inward objective: the desire for God.

The holy Scriptures tell us that we were created by God and thus made for God alone. Slowly we begin to understand the deep craving of our hearts for the One who is our life, the sole object of all our wishes. Simplicity points the way for us, indicating that a certain amount of self-stripping must take place for God to be the sole object of our desires. Simplicity, that virtue-quality so loved by the Holy Spirit, allows us to discern everything: our motives, our attitudes, our inward and outward actions, all those things that can be encouragements or obstacles in our quest to free our souls for entry into that holy state of continual and deep longing for God.

In our busy daily lives, the spirit of simplicity encourages the type of inward renunciation that is totally indispensable for journeying towards God. Self-renunciation and a certain detachment are absolutely necessary for us to swim with complete freedom in the deep waters of spiritual struggle. All our efforts toward self-renunciation, self-stripping, are aimed at the removal of the last human resistances and obstructions which will hinder us from being totally free and pure to desire God as our only parcel and good. Simplicity helps to break down the last barriers, the last obstacles, as it purifies and unifies our beings and our motives. Meister Eckhart writes beautifully about the "perfectly simple person," fully present and open to God's will "that his whole happiness consists in being unconscious of his self and its concerns, and being conscious, instead, of God, in knowing nothing and wishing to know nothing except the will and truth of God." When we embrace such simplicity we allow the pouring into our hearts of such a thirst and hunger for God that only his own presence alone can satisfy us.

The first hermit monks and nuns retired to the Egyptian and Palestinian deserts to free themselves from all earthly concerns and cultivate this hunger and desire for God alone. They faced the obstacles that came their way, never giving in to discouragement or loosening of spirit; on the contrary, with enviable tenacity they nurtured and transformed this desire for God into continual prayer, intense mystical prayer, a prayer of fire and lasting union. If we could only learn to pray again as these simple desert monks and nuns did, I often think, how blessed we should be!

In their profound wisdom and great humility, the Desert Fathers practiced true evangelical simplicity for they knew it nurtured in them the pure desire for God. This desire engendered in them the constant remembrance of God, the *Memoria Dei*. In turn, this remembrance was the essential element that fostered and engendered the most pure love of God in their souls. Saint John Climacus, the sixth century Sinai ascetic, gave considerable thought to the question, "Who is the monk wise and faithful?" Saint John enlightens and shows us how these solitary desert monks, by cultivating in their hearts unceasingly the *Memoria Dei*, allowed the mystical fire burning in their hearts to render a unique honor and glory to God.

The practice of evangelical simplicity, of daily living it out, helps to correct all those complications we create in ourselves that often prove themselves real obstacles to our final goals. Through simplicity we discover in ourselves our primary needs, our deepest longings, our insatiable appetite for God. Simplicity nurtures this innate desire for God, which lies hidden in the most secret recesses of our souls. Through simplicity, we are allowed to penetrate these deep recesses and there glimpse the sole object of our desires. How good it feels then to find that the God we desire is not far from us, and that he indeed abides in our innermost as a steadfast companion on the road, as the most delightful guest of our souls. The moment arrives when in total simplicity and peace we acquiesce to this God who is our most precious guest; we surrender to the power of his love, allowing his fire to consume and take complete possession of us. We no longer feel hungry or thirsty now, for he fulfills every inch of our deepest needs and desires. As Saint Bernard, that extraordinary Church father who wrote extensively about the desire for God, explained: "This happens when the good and faithful servant is introduced into his Lord's joy, is inebriated by the richness of God's dwelling. In some wondrous way he forgets himself and, ceasing to belong to himself, passes entirely into God. Adhering to him, he becomes one with him in spirit."

O God, you are my God, I seek you,
my soul thirsts for you;
my flesh faints for you,
as in a dry and weary land where there is no water.
So I have looked upon you in the sanctuary,
beholding your power and glory.

PSALM 63:1–2

Simplicity and Prayer

Then Jesus told them a parable about their need to pray always and not to lose heart.

LUKE 18:1

Christian monastic tradition, inspired by the Gospels, arose in the solitude of the Egyptian and Palestinian deserts out of the need for sacred places where its inhabitants could dedicate themselves exclusively to the pursuit of their inner journey—to a life of continual prayer and contemplation—as they sought to connect directly with God. From the very start, the early monks and nuns strived for a life centered on prayer, where the continual search for God was expressed primarily by the practice of unceasing prayer. They had heard Jesus command in the Gospels to pray always, "pray without ceasing" (1 Thessalonians 5:17), and they took this counsel to heart.

All the other monastic disciplines focus on one thing: facilitating a life of continual, uninterrupted prayer for the monk or nun. Sometimes Christians from other parts of the world succeeded in making a pilgrimage to the deserts to learn from the living example of these ascetics firsthand. What they discovered was a simple Gospel-like lifestyle in which the desert dwellers were involved in the practice of deep prayer and contemplation, a life of silence and renunciation, accepted solely for the pure love of God. They admired the fact that these individual monks and nuns treasured their solitude, their place of stillness, the simplicity and frugality of their lifestyle, and their separation from the outside world. The desert dwellers treasured solitude, because it provided them with the freedom and the means to aspire to a continual state of prayer. They devoted their lives to the toil and work of prayer. Abba Agathon, one of these early desert monks, believed that prayer is the greatest labor. Who has not experienced the distractions, the "enemies, the demons" as Abba Agathon calls them, that want to prevent our prayer and deter our spiritual journey?

Simplicity and prayer are intimately connected. Simplicity, of itself, possesses a sort of contemplative attribute that directs our steps towards the desire for continual prayer. Furthermore, it enlightens our minds with the gift of faith, fixing the eyes of our hearts exclusively on the mystery of God. This act itself becomes pure prayer. This inner simplicity allows us to stand before God humbly, as if we were still small children, and it allows us to enjoy every minute in the presence of our Father. This atmosphere of faith and simplicity during prayer imparts us with the deep realization that we have received everything as pure gift from the one who loves us beyond all measure.

As we grow deeper into this inner disposition, this attitude of simplicity, so does our prayer, sustained and nourished by the action of grace. All is grace, as Thérèse de Lisieux used to say, and this is never more true than during those profound moments of prayer. Simplicity then becomes the very embodiment of this grace, its channel and recipient at the same time. Grace feeds this simplicity of spirit in those who truly seek to please the Lord, which in turn elicits from us the yearning and deep desire for intimate communion with God.

We offer ourselves to God through total simplicity in prayer, placing ourselves at his complete disposal. We are calm and at peace while trying to pray, because in prayer we humbly acknowledge that we are not alone but in God's hands. Prayer implies faith and surrender, sometimes blind surrender, though it becomes a joyful and serene experience. What we really surrender are our insecurities and doubts, our lack of faith, and our incomplete trust in God, things which by their very nature tend to alienate us from God. The soul finds its delight and its true home in simplicity while at prayer. In those who try to pray from the bottom of their hearts, this simplicity acts in such a way that their spirits feel inundated by a hundredfold blessings and the delight they experience during those very intimate moments of communion with God.

I once heard simplicity described as the soul's best friend—a wise and delightful expression, rich in meaning and content. Genuinely spiritual persons truly find an almost "fraternal delight" in simplicity: they come to recognize each other instantly, as if they had known each other for centuries. Simplicity leaves an impression of profound peace and serene calmness in the soul, especially during moments of prayer. Simplicity bestows upon the prayerful soul a gentle and tender inner quality, a quiet imprint of self-effacement that allows the soul to make ample space for God at its very center, where one is more deeply united with God.

It is hard to conceive of a spiritual life or a deep prayerful life without true simplicity of spirit. This inner simplicity purifies the heart and makes it wholly detached, also allowing us to accept the spiritual poverty by which we lovingly surrender completely into God's hands, allowing him to maneuver every detail of our lives. A prayerful simplicity is inspired by an attitude of deep faith, and it is a pure and most precious gift from the Holy Spirit. We only come to understand it during those intimate moments of prayer when we place ourselves completely at God's disposal. In this loving surrender, this deep, simple, and humble submission of the totality of our being to God, the lover of each soul, we feel his holy presence as he envelops us with the gratuitous gift and fullness of himself.

This prayer has great power
which a person makes with all his might.
It makes a sour heart sweet,
a sad heart merry,
a poor heart rich,
a foolish heart wise,
a timid heart brave,
a sick heart well,
a blind heart full of sight,
a cold heart ardent.
It draws down the great God into the little heart,
it drives the hungry soul up into the fullness of God.
It brings together two lovers,
God and the soul.
In a wondrous place where they speak much of love.

MECHTHILDE OF MAGDEBURG

Simplicity and Worship

"God is spirit, and those who worship him must worship in spirit and truth."

JOHN 4:24

In the Gospel of John, Jesus describes in no uncertain terms the type of worship he expects from his followers. As he engages in a long dialogue with the Samaritan woman, he uses the occasion to teach his disciples how they must go about worshipping the Father in heaven. Above all, Jesus reminds his disciples, they must offer pure worship, adoring God in spirit and truth, in *spiritu et veriitate.* When it comes to true worship, we as human beings owe our Creator the ultimate homage. God deserves the purest, the simplest, the deepest form of our worship and adoration. This type of worship is the fruit of a deep faith and profound knowledge of God (as much as we limited creatures can come to know him), and an experiential knowledge that becomes alive through prayer and contemplation.

The monastic tradition of worship has always distinguished itself by its great sobriety, simplicity, dignity, and reverence, and a profound sense of prayer. Anyone who participates in the worship of a monastic community is always deeply impressed by these intangible expressions of the monastic worship. Monks and nuns love the simplicity and sobriety of their daily liturgy, be it a eucharistic celebration or the hours of the Divine Office, what Saint Benedict rightly calls the *Opus Dei.* The liturgy provides for the monastic, as it does for any Christian, direct access to the mystery of God, to this infinite God who otherwise seems so inaccessible to us humans. The simple monastic liturgy is above all the entrance into God's mystery and the experience of his revelation. Entering into the liturgical mystery, the "heavenly Jerusalem," means entering into the mystery of God himself, into the realm of the divine presence. The early Christians, as well as the entire patristic and monastic tradition, were at home and very comfortable with this sense of liturgy as mystery. Whenever they referred to the liturgy, they always designated it as "the divine mysteries." For the early Christians, entering into the "divine mysteries" meant getting access to the saving act of God, which gets renewed at each liturgical celebration and which changes forever the course of human history. When I speak of and refer to simplicity in worship, I bear in mind how much simplicity itself, accompanied by deep faith, can help us rediscover this approach to the divine liturgy as mystery. We are all deeply influenced by the culture of our times, a type of culture that seems permeated by superficial passing values. Simplicity, illumined by faith and prayer, can help cleanse our sight and all our other senses so that we may again be capable of encountering the beauty and transcendence of God in the mystery of the liturgy. Simplicity actualizes our deep spiritual need for sacramental mystery and makes us yearn for the divine encounter that takes place there. Simplicity teaches us not to question our faith and the long liturgical tradition of the Church, but rather directs us to transcend all that is earthly and hollow as we seek to experience the absolute of God, the transcendent God ever present in his own mystery. Time and space seemed to converge at that very moment when God becomes present to his people in the celebration of the divine mysteries. With true simplicity and purity of heart, we then discover Christ's sacramental presence in our midst, as once did the disciples at Emmaus. With the same simplicity and faith, we worship him, adore him, touch him, get awestruck by him, as we are nourished by his Body and Blood in such a way that we can never again be separated from him. As Saint Ambrose, that great father of the Church once proclaimed: "It is in your divine mysteries, O Lord, that I find and encounter You."

Out of our deep need for God, for contact with the divine, many spiritual seekers today are rediscovering their personal need for worship, for adoration, for encountering the holy in a sacred ritual action. For the Christian, this means participating worthily and with inner simplicity in the divine mysteries. The Eucharist has always been the focal point of the life of the Christian. One of the documents from Vatican II calls the Eucharist the "fountain and summit" of the life of the Church. The mystery and celebration of the Eucharist reenacts Christ's saving action in our midst. When we approach him at the sacred table and are fed with the bread and wine, his Body and Blood, we are indeed nourished with the very life of God, with the supreme gift of himself. This divine mystery is so powerful and awesome that it takes a deep faith, a profound humility, and an unclouded simplicity of heart to recognize God's exquisite gift to his children. For God hides his precious gifts from the proud and the mighty of this world, and he reveals himself to the humble and simple of heart and mind, to the "little ones" of the Gospel: ..."I thank you, Father, Lord of heaven and earth, because you have hidden these things from the wise and the intelligent and have revealed them to infants; yes, Father, for such was your gracious will" (Matthew 11:25–26).

Beauty and simplicity are intimately linked in Christian worship. Beauty, the beauty of the place and the ritual, enhances the sacred action, and an attitude of utter simplicity preserves our minds and hearts from useless distractions. There is no doubt that a beautiful, humble, and dignified liturgical action always leads to deeper prayer and contemplation. The beauty expressed in the liturgy is somehow a mirror of the eternal beauty of God. The same thing can be said about simplicity. True simplicity in worship purifies our vision and all our senses, that we may lovingly and freely gaze upon the beauty of the Lord.

> *One thing I asked of the Lord,*
> *that will I seek after:*
> *to live in the house of the Lord*
> *all the days of my life,*
> *to behold the beauty of the Lord,*
> *and to inquire in his temple.*
>
> PSALM 27:4

Simplicity and the Psalms

The Psalms are the true garden of the solitary
and the Scriptures are his paradise.

THOMAS MERTON, *THOUGHTS IN SOLITUDE*

The heart of the monk carries a special affinity for the Psalms. They are his daily bread, after all, for several times a day he stops the usual toiling and working to offer praise and thanksgiving to God through the praying of the Psalms. Day after day, week after week, season after season, the same prayers get repeated over and over in the monastic services, molding the heart and mind of the monk into an act of endless praise. As the days and months go by, more and more the monk sees the words he prays in the Psalms penetrating the flux of time and shaping the flaw of human history. The mighty acts of God, acknowledged, prayed, and praised daily through the Psalms, seem to bring an imperceptible convergence of all things in the heart of the monk, in the Church at large, and in the entire universe. The Psalms point directly and solely to the one final reality: the consummation of all things in Christ.

Throughout the many years of daily reciting and singing the Psalms, they have become very personal to me—my daily bread, so to speak, my daily inner nourishment. Not only do I love to sing them several times daily, but also to ruminate on them throughout the day. They remind me that God is intimately present at this very moment in my life while I am studying, reading, writing, praying, resting, or working, but that always and at all times, he accompanies me, for his love is everlasting (see Psalm 117). As I immerse myself daily in the flowing river of the Psalms, I am immediately absorbed by their level of depth and utter simplicity. The Psalms are pure and very simple poetry, the cry of the heart at a particular moment, the voice of the Spirit praying in us. Thus, they are not complicated to pray. I am totally convinced that to truly and seriously pray the Psalms, one must approach them with humility and a spirit of deep simplicity. The humble and simple of heart have no problem praying the Psalms. To them is given a particular grace for tasting, ruminating, and understanding these words inspired by the Holy Spirit. They have also learned to make them their own. One of the things that I remember vividly from knowing Dorothy Day, someone so humble and of extreme simplicity in her behavior, is how much she loved to pray the Psalms daily. She and I often spoke about the Psalms. During her later years, while she was staying at our small monastery, each morning around five o'clock I would bring her a cup of tea. Invariably, I would find her deeply involved in the prayer of the Psalms. She always repeated how much she needed this, and that without these early hours of prayer, she would not have the strength to accomplish the work of the day.

Christian simplicity—monastic simplicity—is an art in itself. It is all about the art of living, *un art de vivre*, as the French would say. Such simplicity teaches us how to weave the Psalms into our days, to integrate them wisely into our lives. From the early morning when the first rays of the rising sun begin to illumine the universe, the Psalms sung at Lauds, the morning part of the Office, inspire us to raise our hearts in praise to him who is the eternal Sun of Justice. "O Lord, in the morning you hear my voice; in the morning I plead my case to you, and watch" (Psalm 5:4). In all simplicity, through images and symbols, the Psalms recall God's mighty deeds, such as that early Sunday morning when Christ, our true light, rose from the dead. At noontime, after laboring intensely during the morning hours, we take a pause for Sext, the midday hour of prayer, and the Psalms bring us back into God's presence. They comfort us in our daily struggles by providing a welcome solace, a form of rest, to our tired souls and bodies. "Teach me the way I should go, for to you I lift up my soul. Save me, O Lord, from my enemies; I have fled to you for refuge. Teach me to do your will, for you are my God. Let your good spirit lead me on a level path" (Psalm 143:8b–10). At eventide, when the sun starts to decline and the first shadows appear on the surrounding landscape, it is the hour of Vespers, the time of the evening sacrifice, according to the Psalms. It is the fitting time to offer thanksgiving to God for the gifts received during the day. Psalm 141, the traditional evening psalm, has its origins in the worship of the synagogue. It is sung daily at this time in the churches of the East and the West, pleading with earnest simplicity to Christ the Lord to become our evening light and to dispel all darkness from our minds and hearts. "I call upon you, O Lord; come quickly to me; give ear to my voice when I call to you. Let my prayer be counted as incense before you, and the lifting up of my hands as an evening sacrifice" (Psalm 141:1–2). When the quiet of the nighttime arrives, the Psalms of Compline are there to close the day, assuring each of us of God's loving watchfulness during the dark hours. We take leave of the closing day and feel at peace within, for like little children, we have placed ourselves in all simplicity, in the hands of a loving Father. "[E]ven the darkness is not dark to you; the night is as bright as the day, for darkness is as light to you" (Psalm 139:12), and "I will both lie down and sleep in peace; for you alone, O Lord, make me lie down in safety" (Psalm 4:8).

The Psalms possess the timeless appeal of prayer precisely

because of their extreme simplicity and directness. The simple, straightforward words from the Psalms come in handy at any time, on any occasion, in whatever mood we find ourselves. In this sense, the Psalms are for all Christians a true school of prayer. Through the instrumentality of the Psalms, the Holy Spirit inspires us to pray as we ought and need to do at that precise moment. If it is the moment to render glory to God, the Psalms inspire us to praise him. If it is the occasion to beg for pardon, the Psalms teach us to cry out with true repentance. If we are experiencing pain and suffering at the moment, the Psalms show us how to entreat for help. If we are undergoing great temptations, the Psalms provide us the appropriate words to ask for assistance. If it is the moment to offer thanksgiving to God for his mercies and favors, the Psalms inspire us with the adequate words for singing and rejoicing in his presence. No matter what are our sentiments at the moment, the simple and direct words from the Psalms are there to guide us in the ways of prayer.

To pray the Psalms with true simplicity of heart, in *simplicitate cordis*, means to give attention to the words, not only with our minds, but primarily and foremost in the depths of our own hearts. If our hearts are not awakened to the words, symbols, images, forces, and rhythms of the Psalms as we pray them, much of our praying is probably in vain. The Psalms are not meant simply to be repeated in a strange language, mechanically without understanding. On the contrary, the Psalms are alive today and pregnant with meaning. As such, they are meant to be prayed as Jesus prayed them: in all simplicity, in his own native language and, above all, from the depths of his own heart. During those quiet Nazareth years, Jesus learned from his parents to digest and ponder the words of the Psalms, their most intimate meaning, within the enclosure of his own heart. It was from the depths of his heart that Jesus offered continual praise and thanksgiving to his Father while uttering the words inspired by the Holy Spirit. The praying of the Psalms, these Spirit-filled prayer-poems, were simply his daily tool, part of his daily activity and method of prayer, for offering God a perfect sacrifice of simplicity and praise."Behold, oh God, I have come to do your will."

To end this essay on a practical note, I simply wish to remind the reader that the Psalms were inspired by the Holy Spirit as prayer-poetry to be sung in praise of God. They achieve their full meaning when they are sung, as was the practice of the synagogue and the early church. It has also always been the traditional custom of monasteries, throughout the ages, to sing the Psalms rather than merely recite them. Even today, in most parishes, the Responsorial Psalm after the reading is almost always sung. As Saint Augustine used to say: "He who sings, prays twice." It is not always as important how beautifully they are sung (although this can be very inspiring and nurturing for one's own prayer and for that of the listeners), but that they be sung with true simplicity of melody and form, and always prayerfully, fervently.

Praise the Lord!
Sing to the Lord a new song,
his praise in the assembly of the faithful.
Let Israel be glad in its Maker;
let the children of Zion rejoice in their King.
Let them praise his name with dancing,
making melody to him with tambourine and lyre.

PSALM 149:1–3

Simplicity and Sacred Reading

Deal bountifully with your servant,
so that I may live and observe your word.
Your decrees are my delight,
they are my counsellors.
PSALM 119:17, 24

How often we discover there are instances in our lives when our days are filled not with light, but with bleakness and despair—sickness, violence, tragedy, rejection, loss of someone dear, defeat in our daily tasks, failure in our jobs. These things often seem to be part and parcel of the daily human struggle. There is none among us who at one time or another has not suffered the pains and uncertainties of life. We easily become depressed and distressed under this heavy weight, and we search for light and inspiration to help us in our distress. At times during these dark hours, we find ourselves praying and longing for guidance, for the light, for someone to relieve us from our burdens. To whom shall we make recourse during those moments, except to the Lord who alone controls life's destinies? And who but he alone has the depths of compassion to rescue us and deliver us from our bondage? With the Psalmist we pray: "Out of the depths I cry to you, O Lord. Lord, hear my voice! Let your ears be attentive to the voice of my supplications!" (Psalm 130:1–2).

In the middle of these struggles we begin to understand that peace and enlightenment can only come from God, and more specifically, from listening to the Word of God with deep faith and sensitivity. As the Psalmist poignantly reminds us, "Your word is a lamp to my feet and a light to my path" (Psalm 119:105). It is in the attentive, prayerful reading of God's word that we shall find new resources and strength, that we shall be re-energized and inspired to undertake life's sometimes difficult paths. And we do this with the simplicity of God's children, with a spirit renewed by joy and serenity. True simplicity of heart teaches us that it is through direct contact with God's Word that he becomes the source of our inner healing, the only remedy to our ills, our sole consolation, the one light in our darkness.

The early monks and nuns learned in the desert solitude that their prayer-life depended entirely on their attentiveness to God's Word. Thus they weaved and nourished their daily prayer with frequent reading from the Scriptures. They memorized excerpts from the Bible, especially the Gospels and the Psalms, which they repeated over and over while praying, eating, working, or sleeping. The monks created an inner atmosphere in the depths of their own hearts, an atmosphere of total simplicity and trust, where the contact with God's Word took place quietly, silently. There, with true simplicity, they were fed by God's wisdom as they prayerfully read, pondered, ruminated, tasted, and digested the words from the Scriptures. The more they assimilated the depths and teachings of the Sacred Scriptures, the closer to God they became.

One of the clearest teachings that has remained with me from being nurtured by our predecessors in monastic life, our early desert Fathers and Mothers, is the way they looked at the word of God as the primal nourishment for their spiritual lives. Daily they pondered the Word, and with true simplicity of heart they allowed the Word to dwell in them at all times. They faithfully adhered to Saint Paul's counsel in Colossians 3:16: "Let the word of Christ dwell in you richly." It was through this simple, direct contact with God's Word that the early monks initiated their journey into the mystery of Christ, "the riches of the glory of this mystery, which is Christ in you, the hope of glory," as Saint Paul asserts in Colossians 1:27.

In earlier times, God spoke to the world through the prophets, but in the fullness of time he spoke to us through his only beloved Son, the Word made flesh. Our Christian lives, monastic or otherwise, consists primarily in this attentive listening and pondering of the Word. Through faith we now know that this Word is a living Person; thus he is a living and life-giving Word. During the sublime moment of Christ's baptism, the solemn moment of God's theophany in the New Testament, we hear the Father's admonition: "This is my beloved Son, listen to him." It is a Father's invitation to all of us, his earthly children, to gather together around him who is Truth, the Way, and the Life, and receive him in our hearts as the Word of Life. For as Matthew 4:4 proclaims: "Not on bread alone is man to live, but on every utterance that comes from the mouth of God."

Christian simplicity, simplicity of heart, tells us it is not sufficient just to read or welcome the Word of God; we must also be doers of the word, that is, we must put into practice the teachings contained in God's words. We can only say that we have assimilated and digested God's thoughts and words when they become the flesh of our flesh, when we no longer think by ourselves but think and live as Jesus thought and lived. This is what Saint Paul means when he says: "Put on the Lord Jesus Christ" and "Have in mind that which is in Christ Jesus." A perfect example of all this is Our Lady, Christ's own mother. We read in the Gospels how she received God's Word and kept it in the secret of her own heart in a very simple and straightforward manner. Mary, the humble maiden of Nazareth, did not waste her time in useless speculations about God's message received through an angel, nor tried to feel important at being the receptor of such a privilege. No, she retired into the innermost depths of her own heart where she was most herself and closest to God, and with impeccable humility and charming simplicity, assimilated the Word entrusted to her. Her memory was no longer fixed on the precedent event, the moment of the annunciation, but in the Word that had taken flesh from her and dwelled now in her. One can only try to fathom what attention, what simplicity of spirit, what sort of deep recollection must have enveloped her as she listened and sensed the growth in her of him who is the Word, the Father's eternal Son. During these sacred nine months of her pregnancy, the Virgin maiden of Nazareth became a true "doer of the Word," a perfect example of a silent life of prayer and adoration. Her life is forever marked by this simple reception made in faith and love of God's Word in the depths of her being. So it is that "all generations will call me blessed" (Luke 1:48).

I think there is another important aspect with a subsequent lesson to be learned from this moment of the annunciation, from that unique instant of the Incarnation of God's Son in Mary, which we could find very applicable to our daily *lectio divina*, that is, our approach to the daily reading and pondering of the Scriptures. We must never forget that the sublime act of God's Incarnation is the mysterious work of the Holy Spirit. It is he, with his own divine simplicity, who, in overshadowing Mary, accomplished in her the mystery. Similarly with us, when we daily open the Scriptures and seek to be nourished by God's Word, it is the same Holy Spirit who reveals to us the profound wisdom contained in the sacred pages. It is he and he alone who illumines and gives us the proper understanding of the sometimes hidden meaning implicit in the words. It is by his inspiration and power alone that we learn as Mary once did to ponder and taste the sweet balm found in God's Word. It is the Holy Spirit truly at work in us, the one who opens and simplifies our hearts as he did once with Mary. So too may we receive the light, wisdom, consolation, guidance, and strength that emanates from God's fruitful teachings.

Whenever we seek the proper time for our daily encounter with God's Word, we must always do it in a quiet setting, with a prayerful mind, an attitude of utter simplicity, and complete docility to the inner prompting of the Holy Spirit. In proceeding thusly, we shall receive the divine light from above that clarifies all things during those precious moments of sacred reading, making us see all reality as God sees it. For as Psalm 36:9 points out: "...in your light we see light."

O Lord and Master, You speak to us daily
in an infinite variety of ways. Fill our hearts and minds
with wisdom, simplicity, and divine intuition,
that we may discover you, the inspired and spoken Word,
in the wonders of the Scriptures.
May your words become
our daily bread that nourishes us for eternal life.

BROTHER VICTOR-ANTOINE

Simplicity and the Jesus Prayer

Lord Jesus Christ, Son of God,
have mercy upon me, a sinner.

THE JESUS PRAYER

The connection between evangelical simplicity and the Jesus prayer is an inner one. To truly pray the Jesus prayer, we must first explore the very depths of our hearts, where the action of grace can be felt. There, in the intimacy of our hearts, the Lord has established his own dwelling. Simplicity and interior silence make us aware of this divine presence within. It is from the awareness of this intimate presence within us that our prayer rises as a living whisper to God. Both simplicity and silence allow our minds and emotions to leave behind all other distractions, daily turmoils, and present worries and concerns to concentrate all our faculties and our totally undivided attention on the divine guest who honors our innermost with his presence. Through faith and this attitude of pristine simplicity, we come to understand the Lord's words in the Gospels: "The kingdom of God is among you." We need no longer look for him elsewhere, for he is indeed very close to us, right next to us, very deep within us. And as we try to pray from the depths of our hearts, the Jesus prayer becomes the key that unlocks for us the doors to the wonders of the kingdom within.

Throughout the years, I have learned to approach the Jesus prayer in two ways, as a pilgrimage and with an attitude of Gospel simplicity. The experience of the Jesus prayer in our earthly pilgrimage allows one to be rooted in the "here and now," in the "eternal present," which in turn looks to its consummation in God's eternity. The Jesus prayer is that precious link that connects and gives coherence and consistency to all life stages as they progress towards the eternal. Simplicity has its own role in this progression, for it is that particular Gospel attitude that informs our minds and hearts of how to pray and enter into the prayer itself. In simplicity we say the prayer with our entire being, and yet do not become aware of what we are actually praying. Thus we absorb all the prayer's hidden riches. Gospel simplicity transforms all our senses, all our past memories and present feelings, including our innermost perceptions. It quietly reminds us of only one thing, the presence of the Holy Spirit at work praying in us.

During those moments of intimate prayer, the Holy Spirit takes possession of our souls through his grace. His wonderful grace alerts us that we no longer belong to ourselves, but wholly to God alone. And as we struggled to pray, we are reminded of the apostles' words ,that it is only through the power of the Holy Spirit that we are able to say or pray the sacred name of Jesus (see 1 Corinthians 12:3). As Archimandrite Sophrony, a monastic father from our own times, explicitly tells us: "True prayer to the true God is contact with the Divine Spirit which prays in us. The *Spirit* gives us to know God. The *Spirit* draws us to contemplation of eternity." Therefore, we often cry, "*Veni, Sancte Spiritus!*" begging the Spirit to help us pray.

The Jesus Prayer has its origins in the Gospels. It is the original cry from the Publican: "*Kyrie eleison*...Lord, have mercy" (see Luke 18:13). The prayer, as it evolved throughout the centuries in the desert monastic tradition, gradually incorporated the Holy Name of Jesus itself and hence has become known as the Jesus Prayer. The prayer may be said in many ways, but basically it consists of this very simple form: "Lord Jesus Christ, Son of God, have mercy upon me, a sinner." Could we ever find a prayer of greater depth, truth, and of such utter simplicity? It is one of the charms of the prayer, a prayer of such brevity, yet so direct and containing such a wealth within it.

The secret of the prayer lies in the sweet name of Jesus. Just pronouncing the Lord's name fills us with a unique feeling of recollection and great peace, a peace that surpasses any earthly explanation and signifies to me his real presence in us. For this reason, the prayer has become throughout the centuries a favorite method of praying for many monks and nuns, as well as for millions of lay Christians who have discovered the power contained in the continual recitation of the sacred name. As an old monk used to quietly remind me: "In the prayer of the heart (as the Jesus prayer is also known), I have found my true rest, the place of my repose." He found in the continual recitation of the prayer not only rest, but also peace, consolation, strength, the secret to the practice of unceasing prayer; indeed, he found in the stillness produced by the prayer the very presence of the Lord himself.

One of the reasons that the Jesus prayer is a consoling prayer is that it is also a prayer of humble repentance. It allows us to encounter the Lord and cast our glance upon him in the present state in which we find ourselves: as sinners. There is no room for pretension or grandstanding in the prayer. It is the prayer of the Publican, all of us, who acknowledge our sinfulness before the Lord. Only by presenting ourselves before God as repentant sinners do we gain access to his infinite mercy. Repentance is not an easy task or experience, and it is not always to easy to chat about. Our world today, just like in the times of Jesus, has a hard time trying to apprehend the mystery of repentance. Nor does it grasp its Gospel significance. We live in a society that pretends to be just and virtuous. We are so self-righteous that we would consider it an insult if anyone called us or considered us sinners. And yet the Jesus prayer has its very origins in the humble act of repentance, and it demands true repentance from us as we try to pray. As we enter into the prayer, we acknowledge our sinfulness with great simplicity, and thus we pray to repent for the actual sins of our past and present life. Furthermore, we pray that the Holy Spirit may grant us the grace to repent with our whole being.

While we are in this life, repentance is the secret door to the Jesus Prayer. We need not go too far to enter into it and make it our own. All true prayer begins there, in the very place where we actually stand. And that very real place, our sinful state, is where God is ready to meet us, to welcome us, to forgive us. All we need then is to enter into ourselves with great simplicity and cry out with humble repentance: "Lord Jesus Christ, Son of God, have mercy on me, a sinner." The more often we do this, the sooner and the better we shall discover God's gracious and loving presence in us. The more wholly the mystery of repentance grasps our inner selves, the more we shall be able to behold Christ and cling to his saving garment. During our earthly pilgrimage, as we walk the humble way of repentance while all along never ceasing to pray the sacred name, the more the Lord Jesus becomes present to us. He becomes then our sole reality, our intimate friend, and the one straight path to the Father, for "No one comes to the Father except through me" (John 14:6).

Lord Jesus Christ, Son of God,
have mercy upon me, a sinner.

THE JESUS PRAYER

Simplicity and the Work of Repentance

God, do not spurn a broken, humbled heart.
PSALM 50:19 (*NAB*)

As I write this, it just happens that we are entering into the most blessed period of Great Lent, the appointed time for conversion, for repentance. As I pray and feed daily from the glorious odes and canticles that make the Great Canon of Saint Andrew of Crete, including the life of Saint Mary of Egypt which is an integral part of the Great Canon, I can't help but grow in awareness of the mystery of repentance in our Christian lives, of the immense role it plays in all authentic spiritual life. At the very beginning of our Lenten journey, on Ash Wednesday, as the priest or deacon marks our foreheads with the ashes, we hear Jesus' invitation expressed directly to each of us: "'...repent, and believe in the good news'" (Mark 1:15). This invitation from Christ, so short and direct and uttered in typical evangelical simplicity, is a straight appeal to repentance, to true conversion of the heart.

If we look at repentance with genuine simplicity, in the same way Jesus utters his invitation to each of us, we shall discover in the mystery and character of repentance a great treasure. For contrary to the many negative notions or conceptions one may hold about repentance, there is nothing pessimistic about it. Repentance is instead an invitation to true inner freedom, the type of freedom that only Christ can bestow upon each of us. Repentance is the "prerequisite" that opens for us the doors of the narrow gate that leads to eternal life. "How narrow the gate and constricted the road that leads to life" (Matthew 7:14, *NAB*).

One may ask: What is the connection between simplicity and repentance or, in any case, why try to associate two distinct concepts, two different realities? What does simplicity have to do with repentance? To start, simplicity impregnates in us a clear, single-minded sense of purpose. And this single-minded sense of purpose is the basis or foundation upon which to embark on the path to conversion and true repentance. Repentance is a great mystery, for I see it as the meeting point between two opposites: our utter sinfulness and the unconditional, infinite mercy of God. They manage to come together through the mystery of God's bottomless love. Repentance, when undertaken seriously through the inspiration of the Holy Spirit, is such a positive force in one's life. The early Desert Fathers and Mothers placed the mystery of repentance at the very foundation of one's spiritual life, one's spiritual journey. For them, the mystery of repentance implied not only renunciation of sin and all its consequences, but a complete return to full communion with God.

But what do conversion and repentance really mean? According to Saint Benedict, who followed faithfully the Gospel path and the teachings of the earlier monastic Fathers, conversion means to seek God above all things. It means turning away from our previous life habits in order to return wholeheartedly to him who is the only reason for our lives. Repentance, for the ancient Fathers, meant the radical choice of God alone. With great simplicity, those early Fathers and Mothers made the conscious choice to walk with God alone, to remain docile and faithful to the teachings of their Lord and Master, our Savior, Jesus Christ. For them, to be converted and to embrace the mystery of repentance all started with the deep sorrowful cry from their hearts which acknowledged their sinfulness, their complete failure in the following of God's commands.

Simplicity of the heart, authentic simplicity that reflects genuine Gospel values, is somehow the best preparation for undertaking the work of repentance. Simplicity makes us face straightforward the reality of conversion and repentance. Simplicity tells us in so many words, from the heart, that repentance comes slowly, that it is essentially the work of a lifetime. So to start with, let's dispel all illusions about an easy and comfortable way to undergo a conversion. Repentance means change, and change does not come readily to any of us; after all, we are creatures of habit, good and bad ones, and change is the last thing we wish to impose upon ourselves. Repentance stirs in us the awareness that we must work at changing ourselves daily, and that this effort must include every aspect of our lives, even the smallest and the most concealed or secret ones. Repentance is an inexorable process from which there is no escape or relaxation. Guided by the impulses of grace, humbly and with great simplicity, we accept that we must learn to live according to the laws of God's spirit. The old man in us does not wish to relinquish his prerogatives, and the devil cannot be conquered without doing much battle with him through prayer and fasting. Truly, in the words of the Gospel, we must accept the fact that "the kingdom of heaven has suffered violence, and the violent take it by force" (Matthew 11:12).

Authentic repentance, in its most naked form, consists of a true "therapy of the heart." It is the human heart, the creation and special object of God's infinite love, that needs to be converted, changed, made new, and returned wholly to him. As our hearts grow deeper and deeper into the mystery of repentance, they begin to be purified of their passions, their selfishness, and their self-centeredness. These are the residue of original sin in us—that concrete evil that needs to be wiped out—for it is totally incompatible with the new life of grace we wish to find in our communion with God. The day shall arrive when divine love gets hold of our hearts and possesses them entirely. Then and only then shall we no longer live according to our egotistic passions, our selfishness, and our self-indulgences. In the meantime, while awaiting that blessed day of total liberation, we must renounce humbly all that which is an obstacle for the life of God to grow and expand in us. The more we repent, the greater and deeper the renunciation of the evil that still remains in us, and the deeper this self-renunciation, the more the love of God grows and takes complete hold of us.

If we find the work of repentance painful and get discouraged by it from time to time, let us remember firmly that this stripping of our old selves is a must, a true requirement for attaining eternal life with God. If the process of conversion and repentance gets tedious and arduous, as it should, let us remember that humble repentance is the way of the Gospel. It is the surest way of ascending to God. At times we may find ourselves in a state of total existential stillness, of unbearable darkness, as we continue with our earthly pilgrimage and the unceasing work of repentance. But in the midst of it all, we are reassured by the promise of light at the end of the tunnel. For Christ is patiently waiting for us, and he is the light, the way, and the life. He is the door that opens wide into the glorious kingdom of his Father, our true home and the place of our eternal repose.

Have mercy on me, O God,
according to your steadfast love;
according to your abundant mercy
blot out my transgressions.
Wash me thoroughly from my iniquity,
and cleanse me from my sin.

PSALM 50

PART THREE

Simplicity in Everyday Life

Simplicity and Wisdom

The virtue of wisdom more than anything else
contains a divine element which always remains.

PLATO, *THE REPUBLIC*

Wisdom is a pure gift from God. It is considered one of the seven gifts of the Holy Spirit. And it is through this unique gift that the Holy Spirit allows us to enter into the mystery of God's trinitarian life. Through divine wisdom, the Holy Spirit gives us a glimpse into the very thought of God, into what the intimate divine life is all about, and shows us the way we can approach it from our earthly dwelling. God is most generous with his gifts, and when he bestows upon someone this extraordinary gift of wisdom, it is because he invites that someone to share most intimately into his divine life. As we begin to share the mystery of this divine life, as much as is possible on earth for us mortals, we slowly begin to understand something of the reality of God and his universe as he created it.

Of course, wisdom only gives us a small glimpse of it, for the reality of God is far beyond all human comprehension, all human knowledge, all human understanding. If anything is at all possible in this domain, divine wisdom, which is granted gratuitously by God to souls who are clothed in love, simplicity, and humility, allows a human being to come into contact with the divine Persons in the intimacy of his or her own heart. There, in that intimacy, something of the divine mystery is revealed. A loving intuition is given, something which can never be described in human terms. In the end, all human obstacles disappear and the Holy Spirit leads us to connect directly with God, but this happens only in someone who is already possessed by divine love and clothed in pure simplicity. God loves to grant the gift of wisdom to those who are already longing for his presence, to those who retain lovingly and constantly the memory of God, the *memoria Dei*, and to those who approach him humbly, with simple and grateful hearts.

To speak about divine wisdom in human terms is difficult. It all seems so far beyond us, and in many ways, it is. But what we can do is to speak of the role simplicity plays in leading us into the mysterious ways of wisdom. Simplicity and humility are so basic in spiritual life because they free the human heart to welcome God in his mystery, as he is, beyond all human understanding and categories and as he wishes to reveal himself to us. Nothing is more repugnant to God than the false images we make of him, the crooked concepts we have of him. As Yad Yesode HaTorah describes in the *Maimonides*, "the foundation and pillar of wisdom is to recognize that there is an original Being...and that all exist only through the reality of his being." The Lord loves those of simple hearts because, contrary to others, they refuse to categorize the idea of God in one way or another. For them, the God of the Bible is "he who is," the eternal being beyond all comprehension and description.

What the wisdom from simplicity offers us daily is the aim and desire to live life fully and deeply by allowing us to stand at all times in the immediacy of the divine presence. Wisdom and simplicity enlighten each other, sympathize with each other, and complement each other in that particular co-existence which is each of us alone. Simplicity enlightens our darkness; it brings us out of it by fostering in us a particular sensitivity towards the divine presence, making us realize that at all times and in all circumstances, we stand in the presence of the living God. As Saint

Paul reminds us, "In him we live and move and have our being..." (Acts 17:28). And while simplicity inspires this special awareness, wisdom informs and cultivates in us the constant loving attention we must bestow to the Lord's presence. Simplicity, by fostering this special awareness of God's presence so near to us, unfolds before our eyes the enchantment, reverence, and awe of beholding God in his own mystery. For its part, wisdom implants in us the stillness and special receptivity needed to welcome and embrace this divine guest in the intimacy of our innermost.

Wisdom primarily infuses in us the constant awareness of God; yet it never divorces us from other human concerns, from the travails and pains of other people, from the sorrows and anguish in which our present world is engulfed. The simplicity of wisdom urges us to embrace the suffering of others with the depth of compassion shown by Jesus to those who suffered. Wisdom brings upon all of us immense challenges, for the more fervently we seek it, the greater our challenges. Wisdom is never a passive state of affairs, but rather a way of being; a way of perceiving all reality; a way of acquiring true knowledge; a way of balancing all the diverse components of our lives; and especially, a way of responding to others as we would respond to God himself. Simplicity, integrity, compassion, forgiveness, selflessness, and empathy for others are all attributes of a life immersed in divine wisdom and possessed by the Spirit of God. Ultimately, divine wisdom enlarges our hearts to carry within it all the pains and joys found in our world today. Wisdom embraces all of it through the depths of knowledge, love, and compassion that spring forth from the heart of God.

Wisdom, something often totally different from human knowledge, is indeed a pure gift from God. We can never acquire it on our own. We can only prepare ourselves through the practice of simplicity, prayer, and all the rest of the virtues for the time when the Lord may wish to infuse our souls with this divine gift. When the Spirit of God bestows the gift of wisdom upon us—this fathomless treasure of the spiritual life—countless blessings accompany it.

By embracing and walking the paths of simplicity, we are moved more and more to reject the false values of this world, those things in the culture that alienate us from God. Simplicity trains our minds to believe that "only one thing is necessary." Thus, simplicity moves our minds beyond the realm of pure human thought and human reasoning, and it is then when wisdom instigates in us the new way of thinking of which Saint Paul speaks of when he asserts that we are a new reality in Christ. This new way of thinking, fraught with wisdom, makes us contemplate God alone, ponder his presence at all times and in all places, and allows us to find all our delight and joy in him. As we ponder the bliss of this divine presence in us, we are motivated to love him wholly, as God alone must be loved. Divine wisdom, a pure and gratuitous gift from above, reveals to us that if we want God to be all in all of our lives, our simple and grateful hearts must remain always there, in him, where our true treasure lies.

O Wisdom, who proceeds from the mouth of the Most High!
Reaching out mightily from end to end,
And sweetly arranging all things:
Come to teach us the way of prudence.

O *SAPIENTIA*, VESPERS LITURGY FOR DECEMBER 17

Simplicity of the Ordinary

I will walk with integrity of heart
within my house...
PSALM 101:2

The virtue of simplicity and the unfolding of the ordinary in our lives are like first cousins: they are closely related. In its own quiet way, simplicity enlightens and gives meaning to the most trivial activities of what many may consider a very plain human existence. I always make the effort to give extra credit to simplicity and weave it into the fabric of our daily chores, whatever they may be, for I find it to be an important milestone of our otherwise very ordinary spiritual journey. How impoverished we would be in the daily events and ordinary maturing of our lives without the help and discipline of Gospel simplicity!

One of the particular gifts attached to the inclusion of simplicity into our daily lives is that it facilitates in us a return to our very center, that hidden place where we can cultivate a loving attention to God's presence in the midst of the most mundane occupations. We may at times be very busy and find ourselves longing for some spiritual relief. Suddenly, a simple glance at an icon, a crucifix, a lovely tree, a cloudless sky, a flower, or a sunset—and that simple act empowers us to regain our center. It provides us the needed support for continuing the task, our inward journey, and hopefully brings it to a successful completion.

The more seriously we approach the theme of Gospel simplicity, the more convinced we become of its intrinsic value as vital antidote to some of our contemporary ills. Three or more of the most negative aspects of contemporary culture (just to name a few) are the tendencies toward complexity, stress, and fragmented living, all of which often bring with them a profound sense of boredom. These salient attitudes resurface again and again in our present culture and in the everyday lives of our people, especially the young. They squarely point to the fact that often the choice we make is not for the freedom we proclaim, but rather for a form of slavery we embrace.

Complexity, stress, and boredom are nothing else but the deep symptoms of the sort of fragmented living so prevalent in our times. The accumulations of activities, stressful work, tense relationships, possessions, and busy schedules tend to have a direct correlation with a type of human existence that becomes ever more cluttered by day and that lacks, deep down, a unifying center. The Gospel tells us that we usually reap what we sow. If we continue to sow the negative seeds of destruction, stress, depression, and compulsive greed, then we should not be surprised by the fruits we reap.

Unfortunately, we all know many people caught in this lifestyle, and as a consequence, they seem to find little satisfaction in their personal lives. Once, a wealthy, busy man who spent some time in the monastery guesthouse told me, "A bored, cluttered, materialistic form of human existence is not a blessing for anyone, but more of a curse and source of unhappiness." People immersed in this form of lifestyle find great discomfort and extreme boredom in the smallest incidents—incidents that to others may be a source of true contentment. It is the attitude of basic simplicity (or the lack of it) that makes the difference between those who experience boredom and dissatisfaction in the midst of such incidents and those who would consider them special gifts in their ordinary day. For those who deliberately make the choice of embracing simplicity as a lifestyle, what matters the most is not success or the accomplishment of big things, but the freedom and the joy they find in allowing themselves to be shaped by the small events of their routine. Like Jesus, the Master, we the disciples can make our ordinary, uneventful daily lives a special place where we encounter the Father. It can be a place where we experience real freedom and profound joy. Incorporating Gospel simplicity into our daily lives means that we are truly determined to choose only those things that are essential for the journey, the things that truly matter for a healthy spiritual life. To the rest we cheerfully say, "Enough, I no longer have need of you." Acting upon our resolve, we discard them as totally unnecessary.

As we pattern our ordinary activities with simplicity of heart, we remember that it is God who ultimately shapes our daily lives according to his loving plans. He has a plan for each of our lives, and by living simply, sanely, and humbly, we allow him to shape our lives according to his mysterious designs. Thus, the ordinary stuff of our routine, imbued by Gospel simplicity, becomes a channel of his grace, a loving invitation to enter into full communion with him who is Father, Son, and Holy Spirit.

Lord God,
Bless this day, and by the power of your grace
enable me to speak at all times
of your power and glory.
Inspire me to serve you with a pure spirit,
with simplicity, humility, patience, and love.

BROTHER VICTOR-ANTOINE

Simplicity and the Present Moment

O that today you would listen to his voice!
Do not harden your hearts, as at Meribah...

PSALM 95:7-8

The burden of our daily duties, as well as the mental and psychological burdens that often spring from our concerns and worries, can sometimes distract us from keeping the memory of God alive in the intimacy of our hearts. Life becomes so complicated at times that seldom do we take time to withdraw to a quiet place, as Jesus often did, to recapture our spiritual equilibrium. Our daily worries have such an impact in our psyches, in our lives, that sometimes as we project a future solution to them, we altogether forget to make the most of the present moment—the here and now—allotted to us by God.

Today, with all of us caught up in our so-called "careers," trying to make a living for ourselves and our families, we are confronted with the problem of "busy-ness," what is often called the "sickness of our times." This relentless busy-ness seems to overcome us all. Our lives often seem to lack direction; we are made to go around and around endlessly, nonstop from morning till night, without a sense of purpose as to where we are heading. As we experience this sense of meaninglessness, we often get depressed and are overwhelmed by a certain fatigue. These are chronic symptoms of a life that has lost its balance, its center, its sense of aim. It is often very difficult to escape a chronic situation such as the one described here. What can we do then? How can we re-invent our lives from another perspective?

For those spiritually inclined and who cultivate seriously the desire for God, there is hope and help on the way. We can start by looking at the life of Jesus in the Gospels and learn from his example. One of the first things we notice is the striking simplicity of his ways, his behavior, and his teachings. He makes radical simplicity a mark of true discipleship. He not only teaches about simplicity, but he encourages his disciples to practice it: "Look at the birds of the air; they neither sow nor reap nor gather into barns, and yet your heavenly Father feeds them. Are you not of more value than they? And can any of you by worrying add a single hour to your span of life?" (Matthew 6:26–27).

In the biblical passage quoted above, we perceive Jesus teaching to his disciples two very concrete lessons in Gospel living: simplicity and attention to the present moment. He tells them that tomorrow will take care of itself. We realize that it is all about today, the today of God, that we must be concerned. This simplicity of mind and heart, of lifestyle, allows us to rediscover the presence of God in the immediacy of the present moment, the very moment in time our lives unfold. Jesus firmly teaches us, and we are also thus reminded by the Desert Fathers and Mothers not to look for God elsewhere or at other times. Instead, we are all invited now, at this very moment, to meet and encounter God today and listen to his voice. Our bodies and minds may find themselves engrossed in multiple tasks, but through inward simplicity, both mind and heart can find their way back to the heart of God. God is the center of our being, and it is toward him alone that we must gravitate at all times, constantly, and in all occasions. Nothing is more important than that.

At times, in the midst of endless occupations, we may try to escape the burden they bring by making other plans and rearranging our future. However, if we try to live in the present moment, we realize the future does not yet exist. Simplicity makes us aware that we only have the present, that this present moment is terribly important and most intensely vital to our spiritual journey. The present moment is the time chosen by God to give himself to us. It is today that we are invited to listen and ascertain his voice. It is now that we must open up our empty hearts in sincere offering to him. It is easy to look back on the past and all its intricacies, as it is easy to make plans for the future and all its uncertainties. However, Gospel simplicity is there to remind us we no longer possess the past, our yesterdays are done and gone and our tomorrows are in the hand of God. Simplicity asserts once and for all times that we only have the present, that we are only alive in the present. We must be careful not to waste the present hours, for they belong to God. Our God is the God of the present, of the here and now, and it is at that precise moment that we are invited to dwell and be united with him.

Lord, our God, You invite us daily
to enter into the mystery of your presence.
You transcend time and space
and dwell in the eternal now.
May your peace, which transcends all understanding,
keep us rooted in the knowledge and love of your only Son,
Our Lord Jesus Christ.

BROTHER VICTOR-ANTOINE

Simplicity and Work

You must learn to be still in the midst of activity
and to be vibrantly alive in repose.

INDIRA GANDHI

Work in any form is an integral part of all human life. It is the same reality inside or outside a monastery. We are all conditioned to work and to live from the results of our work.

While work can be considered a universal aspect of all human existence, it is nevertheless today a complex issue to talk or write about. The concept of human work, the humble task of earning our daily keep and living as taught in the Scriptures, has evolved so much in our culture in past decades that when other people discuss the subject I often wonder if we are talking about the same thing. The concept of work ends up having many meanings these days, as numerous as all the types and varieties of work there are in our large society.

One of the sad things I notice while observing our present society is how something as good as the reality of work has nevertheless degenerated into something else. We are very distant these days from its functional concept in the Bible, from the very example of Jesus, Saint Joseph, and the Apostles themselves, who labored with their hands to earn a simple living. Today, the concept of human work is grossly misinterpreted. It is no longer simply a means of humbly supporting oneself. Guided by the false values of a culture that places so much emphasis on greed, materialism, self-fulfillment, possessions, and pleasure, human work has in some cases been transformed into something of a monstrosity.

In the past, human work was able to safeguard its own dignity by placing the emphasis on the fact that one worked in order to live. Today the reverse is true: we live to work, motivated by the desire to achieve and obtain all the things mentioned above.

In the past, human work was looked upon as necessary for supporting oneself or one's family. Today work is seen more as a career, a way to success, a means of becoming wealthier and possessing more. Often, greed is the ultimate goal. How, otherwise, can one justify the obscene salaries of the so-called CEOs of our times, when others don't earn the minimum for human subsistence? For those who believe, the Gospels express strong warnings against this very prevalent attitude of our times: "'For what will it profit them to gain the whole world and forfeit their life? Indeed, what can they give in return for their life? Those who are ashamed of me and of my words in this adulterous and sinful generation, of them the Son of Man will also be ashamed when he comes in the glory of his Father with the holy angels'" (Mark 8:36–38).

When I first conceived of writing about the relationship of simplicity and daily work, I never intended to present the idea of work as I did here. But as I thought and prayed more about it, I realized that as complex as the subject is today, I couldn't avoid it altogether. *If I speak of work, of what type of work am I speaking?* I asked myself. Inept as I am on the subject of contemporary forms of work and labor, they must somehow be included here, and perhaps the Holy Spirit may shed some light in our darkness. It is easier for me to speak about daily monastic work, but small and humble as this little book may be, it is not only for monks and nuns, but for all those of goodwill who may wish to incorporate Christian simplicity into their daily routine. That, of course, includes work.

Saint Benedict, a true master of the monastic life, envisions the life of his monks and nuns as one where there is sufficient balance between the activities of prayer, work, rest, eating, reading, and study. In writing his *Rule* and counseling his monks, he aimed at moderation, balance, and equilibrium in all things. This is the basic wisdom of his *Rule* and the reason perhaps why it has survived more than fifteen centuries! The monk or the nun, guided by the authority of an abbot or abbess, in harmony with the community, must learn daily to manage time wisely and with utmost care. The concept of work is thus inserted into that of time and closely allied to it. Managing time correctly entails making a list of our priorities at work and concentrating our energies and attention on them exclusively, leaving other cares behind.

Simplicity can be a great help in achieving this goal of balance at work, in our ordinary tasks, and also between work and the rest of our other activities. Simplicity can guide us to determine the most important aspects or tasks of our day's work and how we can go about accomplishing them. For instance, if we work in an office where there is too much noise, clutter, and chitchatting, simplicity may inspire us to avoid all non-essentials and distractions in order to concentrate fully on the task assigned. We might choose silence as a friend and a companion so that we may execute the task on time and in good fashion. Holy simplicity, human simplicity, is always a good mentor to have as we try to manage time, energy, concentration, and other challenges at work. In the nineteenth century, Henry Thoreau wrote something timeless and still appropriate for today: "Simplicity, simplicity, simplicity! I say, let your affairs be as two or three, and not a hundred or a thousand; instead of a million count half a dozen, and keep your accounts on your thumb-nail." Simplicity has its own way of inspiring balance and harmony in the midst of all our activities, even sometimes when chaos seems close at hand. Simplicity is always there to safeguard us, to inspire us, even to protect us.

An important factor to keep in mind is that there must be a certain harmony between our work and the rest of our daily living. It is not unusual to hear someone say, "I hate my job....I don't know why I stay with it." Sadly enough, we can be tempted to sacrifice happiness and well-being for purely materialistic or advantageous reasons. In such cases, inward simplicity can come to our help, inspiring us to re-evaluate our priorities and make the right choices so that we can coordinate our work with our own personal lives. Work, somehow, must be incorporated and made to fit harmoniously with the rest of life, not to exist in opposition to it.

By seeking to simplify our daily living, including our work, we indeed try to recapture the inner harmony that was intended by God for all human existence. From the very beginning of creation, we see that God made us to live in harmony with him, with ourselves, and with all that surrounds us. That initial harmony is there for us to regain through a form of daily living in consonance with God's purpose. Human work may be a burden at times, but it is never meant to be a destructive force of our own inner lives.

If a certain job or type of work is harmful to our spiritual lives, I would say without hesitation, "Quit it; leave it." One of the aspects to watch for is the right use of time. No point in wasting time or energies in something that brings our own spiritual ruin. We must learn to give adequate quality time to our tasks without overdoing it. Often, so little time remains for the rest of our one's interests and activities because he or she is working "overtime." If that happens often, then we must in all simplicity be on the watch.

Vigilance is a must to lead a well-ordered and purposeful life. To achieve a balance, we must not give more time than is normally allotted to our jobs. We must never be consumed by our work, for that would mean we are turning our work into a form of slavery or tyranny. Simplicity should give us the clear perspective to arrange the hours assigned to our daily work in a way that they don't leave aside other equally important activities in our daily lives. If most of our time is consumed by work, where are we going to find time in the day for other tasks we may wish to accomplish like reading, studying, praying, visiting family and friends, and basic leisure? Learning to manage our time properly, in all occasions and circumstances, is one of the lessons we can learn from the wisdom of inward simplicity.

Work is an inescapable feature of our human existence. But we must learn to approach it with the wisdom that comes from simplicity, with true humility, and with a great deal of realism and common sense. We must not sacrifice the rest of our lives to work; we must always try to put it in the proper context. Placed in its proper context and experienced harmoniously with all the other aspects of our lives, work can indeed be a source of wholeness, holiness, health, and contentment. We must raise work from the pragmatic level of just providing our daily support to one that fosters true humanness and brings inner joy into our lives. To accomplish this we need God's grace, and for that we pray daily, with true simplicity of heart.

In the intimacy of our own hearts, we seek daily your presence, O Lord. For you said to us:

> *"Come to me, all you that are weary and are carrying heavy burdens, and I will give you rest."*
>
> MATTHEW 11:28

Simplicity and Frugality

Find out how much God has given you, and from it take what you need; the remainder which you do not require is needed by others.

SAINT AUGUSTINE

Frugality and simplicity are cherished virtues within the monastic tradition because they come from the teachings of the Gospel and the example of Christ's own life. The first monks and nuns in the desert paid heed to these attractive virtues, leaving to the rest of us their examples and teachings as testaments.

Through the practice of voluntary frugality, we foster in the monastery a certain attitude, a certain philosophy of life, that is radically opposed to the values of present-day society. We view the consumerism encouraged by governments, markets, the media, and certain economists as totally unnecessary, wasteful, and certainly harmful to the life of the spirit. The monk's daily life tries to affirm the truth that we can all live better by learning to live with less, and we deliberately assert our inner freedom by renouncing the slavery of overconsumption.

Voluntary frugality doesn't mean necessarily living in a state of destitution. It means learning to distinguish between the things that we really need in daily life and those that we don't and can do without. It means buying something because it is needed in the monastery, not simply because we personally want it. It means treating objects, tools, and utensils with such respect that they can last more than a lifetime. It means both refusing to take part in any kind of waste and being thrifty enough to recycle most of the products discarded by our materialistic, wasteful society. Ultimately, frugality is a tool that helps us monks place our values, perspectives, and priorities on what is really important, on the one thing necessary.

Many years ago, when we needed to expand a wing of the monastery and didn't have enough material resources, someone offered us all the materials from an old house that was going to be demolished in the nearby village. With the help of a friend, we went about the task of dismantling the floors, doors, closets, windows, wood panels from the walls, and all else that could be reused in the new building. Because the wing was finally built mostly out of these recycled materials, and because some of the work—like stripping the old paint, plastering, painting—was done by ourselves, it ended up costing us less than half of what the normal cost would have been. When it came to furnishing the monastery, we have always relied on the old used furniture given to us by friends or found in the streets of New York and brought here, where we patiently repair, restore, refinish, and put them again to good use. We have a good neighbor who is a professional painter, and he gives us leftover cans of paint and stains. We, in turn, mix the different cans until we have enough to repaint the rooms in need.

When it comes to food, we have a few chickens that provide us and our monastery guests with eggs. A garden provides vegetables during the growing season; we freeze and preserve some for the cold months. Besides the food from our gardens, one of the largest food stores in the country gives us a certain amount of vegetables and fruits that they can't sell, some of which we use to feed the animals, some of which we share with those in need, and some of which we eat ourselves. We do the same with the day-old bread and pastries that the two local bakeries provide. Sometimes we even get cakes, as we did this past Christmas Eve, which we were able to serve afterward to all those who came to attend Christmas Mass.

Monastic life has always, like the Gospels, been countercultural. While society's incentive is to spend, expand, consume, and waste, monastics choose the opposite as a valid alternative: spend and consume less, scale back on your possessions, avoid cluttering, share and give away to others what you don't need, build small dwellings, and conserve energy and other resources. Monks deliberately make the choice of the good life instead of the trendy fast track of our times.

I think the example of monks has something to offer the world, which is largely directed to the slavery of consumption, often at the expense of the poor and the underprivileged of our planet. The monastic lessons of frugality, austerity, sobriety, and productivity have proven to be a more human, more Christ-like and freeing alternative to the seductive, superficial view espoused by a materialistically-oriented world.

Therefore let all who are faithful
offer prayer to you;
at a time of distress, the rush of mighty waters
shall not reach them.
You are a hiding-place for me;
you preserve me from trouble;
you surround me with glad cries of deliverance.

PSALM 32:6–7

Monastic Simplicity

Then Jesus called the twelve together and gave them power and authority over all demons and to cure diseases, and he sent them out to proclaim the kingdom of God and to heal. He said to them, "Take nothing for your journey, no staff, nor bag, nor bread, nor money—not even an extra tunic. Whatever house you enter, stay there, and leave from there. Wherever they do not welcome you, as you are leaving that town shake the dust off your feet as a testimony against them."

LUKE 9:1–5

Simplicity and humility are the hallmarks of an authentic monastic life: they are, so to speak, the feet or pillars on which a true spiritual life stand. The monk, as Saint Benedict indicates, must guide his entire existence by the counsels of the Gospel. The Gospels and the example of Jesus' life must somehow be incorporated into the monk's daily life to such an extent that they become flesh of his very flesh. From the Gospels we learn and see that Jesus was born, lived, worked, preached, and died in great simplicity. Thus, our task, the task of all disciples, is to follow in the footsteps of the Master; for as the Master also reminds us, "A disciple is not above the teacher..." (Matthew 10:24). A complete acceptance of the Gospels, a total immersion in them, therefore implies a conversion and change from our previous lifestyle to one of radical simplicity.

A wise old monk used to tell me "a true monk is always wrapped in simplicity." This total immersion in simplicity, however, is not always easy for the monk to achieve. He must struggle and labor at it daily. From the experiences of everyday living, we learn that our world, our society, our institutions (including the religious ones) are all very complex. At times, we feel manipulated by the present forces that run our world, and our lives seem then totally out of our own control. Often, we feel drawn towards multiple and contradictory things at the same time, and we sense the pressures that descend upon all of us from our diverse cultural, educational, biological, and even spiritual backgrounds. All that which we experience, all that we are, all that surrounds us seems manifold, multiform, too complex and insurmountable.

In our present day, we witness nations at war with one another, we see terror inflicted upon other human beings, we indulge in the propensity to dominate and control other countries and other people's lives. We experience deeply the conflict that permeates our world, the struggle that subsists in ourselves between our own body and the spirit, the tension between our intellect and the heart, the rift between the individual human being and society at large, the strife between humanity and its environment created to nurture us. As we squarely face these realities, we gradually come to the realization that complexity is rooted in the very core of who we are. It is part and parcel of our daily existence, and often, we are unable to handle its weight, its tensions, its chaotic and deadly seeds of destruction.

As we confront such a harsh and crude reality, I am often asked, how does the Christian monk face these perplexities, all these endless conflicts and turmoil? To whom does he look for guidance and resolution of these conflicting tensions? The only answer lies in the total acceptance of the Gospel and its fundamental message of simplicity, based on the life and example of Jesus himself. Monks must always choose to follow the example of Christ and imitate his life. This is what true discipleship is all about. The forms and examples of simplicity after which monks usually pattern their lives are those which Christ used at one time or another during his years in this world. True, inner simplicity is an attitude above all, and the monk seeks to nurture this attitude of simplicity, humility, and obedience until death.

We know from the Gospels that Jesus often did not have a stone or place to lay down his head in repose (see Luke 9:58). Jesus also often fasted and took only what was necessary for the journey. He did not mince or waste words in his interactions with others. He spoke only to teach or to answer questions, and at very important moments in his life, he simply remained silent. Even during his own final entrance into Jerusalem, often portrayed as a triumphal one, Jesus made it most humble and simple. Saint Andrew of Crete tells us: "He comes without pomp or ostentation. As the psalmist says: He will not dispute or raise his voice to make it heard in the streets. He will be meek and humble, and he will make his entry in simplicity." This attitude of simplicity that we see in Christ is an ascetic model not only for the monk, but for every Christian. It is by contemplating Jesus that all of us Christians are able to pattern our own lives after the example and program laid down by the Master.

As disciples of Jesus, the Christian monk strives daily for the single-mindedness taught in the Gospels. In his quest for this blessed state of simplicity, the monk is helped by constant prayer. As he strives daily to practice self-renunciation, he renounces not only himself but also every form of worldly illusion. These ascetic efforts are part of the dying of the self that is a must in order to open our hearts fully and in all simplicity to the power of God acting in us. Our self-centeredness and our obsession with our ego are often the greatest obstacles to the work of the Holy Spirit in us. By accepting our nothingness, by letting go of all our pre-conceived designs and successes, we allow God to move freely into our lives, to intervene in them as he pleases, and finally to rescue us in our hour of despair. It is precisely during these moments when we experience most deeply our nothingness and weaknesses that we feel his saving presence in our lives. With grateful hearts and profound simplicity, we acknowledge in prayer the measure of grace given to us at those very precise and crucial moments.

From the early monastic Fathers and Mothers, and from Saint Benedict himself, the monk learns that by following the Gospel way of self-renunciation he is able to rid himself of all that is superfluous and redundant in his daily monastic life. By embracing the ordinariness of his life with utter simplicity, the monk is able to refute the temptations that come from a world controlled by achievement, power, and illusion. Thomas Merton, in one of his early writings, describes aptly his own conception of monastic simplicity as "the concern with doing ordinary things quietly and perfectly for the glory of God is the beauty of the pure Benedictine life." The daily, the ordinary, the routine: these are the everyday means God uses to lead the monk in the ways of the Gospel.

Practically speaking, the "extraordinary" doesn't exist in a monk's life, except in the sense of the extraordinary way in which he performs his ordinary, regular duties. The monk accepts simplicity as a given in his spiritual journey, for by the very definition of the word monk, *monachos*, it signifies he who is one, alone, single-minded. Complexity, avarice, multiplicity, division, tension, conflict, and chaos are all contrary values to what a humble and well-ordered monastic life is all about. The monk can only achieve peace with himself and his own inner unity when he is free from all redundancy and clothed in true simplicity. He rejoices in Jesus' counsel as he assimilates it into his own life: "'Therefore I tell you, do not worry about your life, what you will eat or what you will drink, or about your body, what you will wear....your heavenly Father knows that you need all these things" (Matthew 6:25, 32). Then he is totally at peace with God, with his environment, with his brothers and sisters and with all that surrounds him. As the course of his life unfolds daily, with child-like simplicity, the monk entrusts his existence, his fears, his basic needs, and everything else to the providence of a loving Father.

The attitude of monastic simplicity, understood thus, becomes and embraces a radical reaction to the false values and security our contemporary world offers. It also becomes a beacon of hope towards reaching and enjoying the true inner freedom God intends for all his children. This attitude directs our hearts and minds—indeed all that we are—toward God, in who alone the integration of all our apparent contradictions can be achieved. Gospel simplicity, accepted and incorporated into monastic daily life, not only liberates the monk from the heavy burden of earthly and material attachments, but frees both his mind and heart to focus on Jesus, his Savior and Master. This Gospel simplicity allows the monk to experience deeply with himself the ultimate transparency of truth: the type of truth of which Jesus spoke when he said, "I am the way, and the truth, and the life" (John 14:6). Monastic simplicity is inspired and embraced by the monk for the pure love of Christ. It is he, ultimately, who can totally purify our hearts and most intimate desires, who can unify our sense of purpose and redirect all our energies towards the realization of the kingdom of God.

You make springs gush forth in the valleys;
they flow between the hills,
giving drink to every wild animal;
the wild asses quench their thirst.
By the streams the birds of the air have their habitation;
they sing among the branches.
From your lofty abode you water the mountains;
the earth is satisfied with the fruit of your work.

You cause the grass to grow for the cattle,
and plants for people to use,
to bring forth food from the earth,
and wine to gladden the human heart,
oil to make the face shine,
and bread to strengthen the human heart.

PSALM 104:10–15

Simplicity and Service

"It will not be so among you; but whoever wishes to be great among you must be your servant, and whoever wishes to be first among you must be your slave; just as the Son of Man came not to be served but to serve, and to give his life a ransom for many."

MATTHEW 20:26–28

The Christian is invited by the Holy Spirit to come to the experiential knowledge that the community we usually call "church," *eklessia*, is not simply a religious institution. It is something greater and much more important than that. It is the Body of Christ, the gathering together of all God's children scattered around the four corners of the world to form together one family, the family of God. This experience of the church as a family makes us realize deeply that we are all bound to one another, as brothers and sisters, because we are all children of the one and same God. When we honor one another, when we render a small service to one another, when we welcome the stranger and pilgrim into our homes, when we care for the suffering and the elderly, the widow and the orphan, it is a member of God's own family we honor, serve, receive, and welcome. Furthermore, since we are all members of the Body of Christ, it is Christ himself (as Saint Benedict assures us) who is being honored, served, and welcomed in the brother or sister we assist.

Jesus never ceases teaching about the nature of genuine service to his disciples. The Gospels are full of examples of this type. Not only does he speak or show by example what evangelical service is all about, but he goes as far as showing himself to be the servant of all. Among all the Gospel texts dealing with this subject there is none more striking, profound, and full of his unique simplicity than the words in John 13:3–15: "Jesus, knowing that the Father had given all things into his hands, and that he had come from God and was going to God, got up from the table, took off his outer robe, and tied a towel around himself. Then he poured water into a basin and began to wash the disciples' feet and to wipe them with the towel that was tied around him" (13:3–5). In this admirable passage from Saint John's Gospel, we learn from Jesus' amazing example the extent to which we as Christians are called to be servants to one another. "'Do you know what I have done to you? You call me Teacher and Lord—and you are right, for that is what I am. So if I, your Lord and Teacher, have washed your feet, you also ought to wash one another's feet. For I have set you an example, that you also should do as I have done to you" (13:12–15). The disciples were left utterly confused by this act, for they had just watched a few days earlier his triumphal entrance into Jerusalem where he was acclaimed as King and Lord. Yet Christ, who was born in humble Bethlehem and spent his growing years in Nazareth in simplicity and service to his parents and neighbors, wished one more time to give to his followers a living example of unconditional love and service.

Those who opposed Jesus during his time of preaching and service, Judas among them, couldn't understand or fathom the true cost of discipleship. Being a disciple is to become the servant of others. By humbly washing the feet of his disciples, Jesus gave not only an example of his admirable humility, but even more so a living example of love, submission and service to one another. And this he did, a few hours before he was apprehended by the soldiers and taken into custody as a criminal, when time was of the essence and nothing else mattered. By this astonishing example of washing the disciples' feet, an action performed with utter simplicity, the Teacher and Master left to us, his followers, a clear pattern of how we also must love and serve one another.

The Gospel teaching about service—that is, Jesus' own radical example and precept that we must be servants to one another—is a huge challenge to every Christian who is serious about putting the Master's words into practice. It is a challenge to live and pray in a new way, the simple Gospel way. It is a challenge to look and see the world through a new lens and follow the example of Jesus by living selflessly. This is what an authentic Christian life is all about. It is a continual challenge to absorb the Master's example by fully embracing a simple life of love and service to other human beings, our brothers and sisters, a life that puts its priority in a complete trust in God and the practice of the command to love one another. No one is exempt from this, not even the most cloistered of monks or hermits. The monks in the desert knew this teaching well and were assiduous in its practice. When someone apologized to them for disturbing them in their solitude or silence, their simple response was, "This is why I am here, to serve you and attend to your needs." What an example of true Gospel simplicity!

True Gospel simplicity teaches us that to serve our brothers and sisters is to serve God himself. The Lord reminds us clearly in the Gospel that what we do to the least of our brothers we do unto him. Our father Saint Benedict absorbed so deeply this Gospel lesson that in chapter 53 of the Rule, which deals with the reception of guests, he tells his monks: "All guests who present themselves to the monastery are to be received as Christ, for he himself said: 'I was a stranger and you welcomed me'" (see Matthew 25:35). Later in the same chapter he adds: "By a bow of the head or by a complete prostration of the body, Christ is to be adored because he is indeed welcome in them." We Christians fulfill the Lord's commandment to love one another by the service and comfort we provide to those near us and in need. The Lord makes sure that we encounter many during our lives who are troubled and suffering, especially the poor and the dispossessed, the hungry and the homeless, the lonely and the depressed. Christ often arrives unannounced to our doors and we must honestly ask ourselves how we should welcome or react to him.

We are not all called by the Lord to save the world, but we are certainly all called to serve one another, in truth and simplicity, after the very example of Christ, our Master and Savior. The Lord invites each of us daily, as workers in his vineyard, to render small services to our neighbor, to work in whatever way possible in service to one another, to alleviate the suffering of those next to us, our brothers and sisters. As Christians, we are all called to walk in the light that shines forth from the Gospel and to be joyful servants, finding our real fulfillment in knowing ourselves servants of the Lord. This is, essentially, what the Gospel lesson of the washing of the feet is all about: authentic Christian love expressed with utter simplicity towards our neighbor.

God of power and mercy,
only with your help
can we lead simple lives of fitting service.
Bless the daily toil of our hands
that we may continually offer your praise
and learn to live by the Gospel faith we profess.

BROTHER VICTOR-ANTOINE

PART FOUR

Simplicity and the Saints

Simplicity and the Mother of God

It is easier to depict the sun with its light and its heat than to tell the story of Mary in its splendor.

JACOB OF SERUG

We as Christians and disciples of Jesus can learn from the simplicity we encounter in Mary, his mother. She is a living example of Gospel simplicity. I would go as far as to assert that she is simplicity personified. The image of Mary, as we capture quietly from the Gospels, stands against all that is false, haughty, selfish, and arrogant. By her presence alone she dissipates the forces of darkness and evil. From the moment she receives the good news from the Archangel Gabriel about the mission God intended for her, she accepts her role with infinite humility and simplicity. She doesn't attribute anything to herself. She is the humble and obedient servant of the Lord. Filled with the beauty and strength of her own simplicity, she accepts lovingly the Lord's design for her: "'Here am I, the servant of the Lord; let it be with me according to your word'" (Luke 1:38). She demands nothing from Gabriel, God's messenger; on the contrary, she accepts everything, and in return she receives everything. The Word becomes flesh in her, and by taking her own flesh, the Son of God becomes also the son of Mary. She who was poor and powerless, the true *anawim,* now possesses all: God himself. From now on, all generations shall call her blessed.

We call her Our Lady, the *Theotokos*, Queen of Heaven, and yet in all her natural simplicity, Mary continues to refer to herself simply as "the servant of the Lord." What profound lessons about true simplicity we can all learn from her! She is not there to prove anything to us, but simply to show us the way to complete surrender and submission to God's will. Like Mary, we too are called daily to utter our fiats not once, but many times. And like Mary, our model of Gospel living, we too must utter these fiats in total simplicity, with complete humility and trust in God's plan for each of us.

Christians, and also many non-Christians, are aware of the unique role that Mary, the Mother of God, plays in the tradition and lives of both Catholics and Orthodox. From the very early days of the primitive Jerusalem church, long before the Apostles dispersed to the four corners of the world to bring the Good News of the Gospel, the veneration of she who gave birth to God, Mary Most Holy, was an integral part of that early Christian community. Some of the early disciples knew Mary personally and kept her loving memory alive among the rapidly increasing number of Jesus' followers. The Gospels describe the unique place assigned to the Mother of God in the unfolding mystery of our salvation. She is present from the very beginning, from the moment of Gabriel's announcement of the glad tidings of the Savior's Incarnation, and she is also present at the end, at the foot of the cross.

The New Testament is quite limited on the facts it gives about Mary, the Mother of God. The Evangelists, Matthew and Luke, relate events concerning the Incarnation and the birth of the Savior in Bethlehem, including some brief information about his growing years in Nazareth. In the Gospel of John, we find brief mentions of Mary: at Cana, and later standing at the foot of the cross. The Acts of the Apostles describes her quiet presence in the midst of the Apostles at that first Pentecost. In the remaining New Testament books, her presence is obscured, if it exists at all. It is not as if the

New Testament or the early church wanted to keep quiet about Mary or her role during those developmental years of the early church. First of all, the evangelist John the Apostle, to whom Jesus entrusted the care of his mother, tells us that there are many things that Jesus did about which little or nothing is written. From this we can logically conclude that there was much more to Mary, the chosen Mother of the Savior, but for whatever reason the evangelists chose simply to keep a respectful silence about her.

In many ways, by telling us so little about Jesus' mother, the sacred writers seem to say a lot. As the old Spanish proverb suggests, "To him of good understanding, few words suffice." Furthermore, the life of the mother was spent in the shadow of the mystery of her divine Son. How could anyone, except the angels perhaps, utter anything about the sublime intimacy that must have existed between these two? One can only get a hint here and there from the way he addressed her respectfully, mannerly, "Woman," or from the way Mary addressed him after he is found in the Temple or during the Cana wedding. So much of what transpired between Jesus and Mary, between Mother and Son, remains as it should: under the veil of lofty mystery.

Our own personal love for Christ and our conception of him ought not be so flimsy as to not detect the depth of feeling that must have existed between Mother and Son. Shouldn't we also try to capture something of that sublime, unique, and tender love experience that existed between them? I tend to think that our very personal love for her son, Jesus, must become the source and reason for the veneration and love we have for Our Lady. In all simplicity, it is through the gift of faith that we come to the knowledge and acceptance of Christ our Savior, and as we discover and fall in love with him who gave his life to save us, we also come to the marvellous discovery of she who gave him that very life by engendering him in time, thus making possible our salvation. Only God, in his boundless love for humankind, could have formulated or imagined such a divine enterprise. *O Magnum Mysterium!*

The veneration of Mary, beginning from the time of the birth of the church itself, clearly permeates the entire history of Christianity. There are some among Christians who may wish to emphasize her perpetual virginity; others her immaculate conception; still others her dormition and glorious assumption to heaven. Some emphasize the fact that she is the *Panagia* or that she is the all-holy one. The most significant role to me, the one that summarizes Mary's privileges and her supreme role in the plan of salvation, is that of the *Theotokos* or "God-bearer." The early church, assembled in solemn council at Ephesus in 431, declared her so. From then on, all Christians, both Eastern and Western, are called to rightly proclaim her the Mother of God, the one who is intimately connected to the mystery of Jesus Christ, her Son, the mystery that was in God's mind before time began. In many ways, as the church develops and continues to grow, it mirrors itself more and more in the image of Mary, the *Theotokos.*

Our Lady becomes, in a sense, the perfect "icon" of what the Church is called to be: a living worship of love and adoration to the truine God. Mary is the one in whom the Holy Spirit was fully at work during and after the Incarnation. As such, the Church today is also called to live by the fullness of the Holy Spirit infused upon her at Pentecost. Mary is also the one in whom the Word, the Father's eternal Son, came to dwell and take flesh and thus through her become himself impregnated in our own humanity. And so the Church is called to transform her own flesh into the very Body of Christ by living daily the truths of the Gospel and witnessing he who deigned to assume our humanity. Mary, the *Theotokos*, by accepting to become the earthly mother of the Father's only begotten Son, shares with him the unique privilege of making Christ, the Word Incarnate, fully present to our world for the sake of our salvation.

The mystery of the *Theotokos* is embedded within the depths of the mystery of her Son, Christ the Lord; therefore, the Blessed Virgin Mary remains very dear to us, his followers. The Christian faithful, in particular monks and nuns immersed in their monastic contemplative silence, ponder daily this mystery with admiration, while all along realizing it is totally beyond their comprehension. Our monasteries and hermitages are usually ornamented with icons of the Mother of God, reminding us of her quiet presence in our midst. In most of her icons, she is portrayed with her own unique simplicity, carrying the child Jesus in her arms. There we are able to perceive that while the eyes of Jesus rest lovingly in all simplicity upon his mother, her gaze, however, is directed tenderly toward us and toward all those who approach him. With her charming incomparable simplicity, Mary shows her Son to each of us, silently whispering in our ears, "Behold your God, who has become a child for you."

In the Gospels as in the icon, the *Theotokos* is always depicted in physical closeness to Jesus and, without the least hesitation, she points directly to him. In her Magnificat, Mary's song of praise, she refers to herself as "God's humble handmaid," showing us the utter depths of a total self-effacing attitude before the immeasurableness of Jesus Christ. She makes no claims to herself. She is only the simple, humble creature who bore him in time, the Son of God. She acknowledges plainly, simply, humbly, that it is God alone who has done great things in her. It is therefore right, Mary would urge, that all our worship and praise be addressed solely to him. It is to him alone, God our Maker, that our obedience and the undivided attention of our hearts belong.

Filled with Gospel simplicity, and through the eyes of faith, we are able to penetrate into the mystery of Christ, Mary's beloved Son. As we enter into the mystery, we rejoice with great joy, "*Cum gaudio magno*!" as we discover that Mary is both God's Mother and also our own. She adopted us at the foot of the cross when Jesus said to her, "Woman, here is your son" (John 19:26). As Jesus entrusts the beloved disciple to the tender care of his mother, so does he also entrust us to her. In the person of John, each of us also becomes a child of Mary. Filled as she is with God's own light, Mary knows God's loving designs for each of us and she whispers them gently, daily, in our ears. She knows God's plans for us, and she also knows our weaknesses, how slow we often are in following God's ways. As a tender and always helpful mother, she is there, very present to us, very close by, always ready to come to our rescue. As the mother she is to each of us, she is more concerned about our eternal salvation than we are ourselves. And her motherly concerns are not only limited to each of us: they extend to the whole world, to the entire universe. Like her son, she is particularly concerned for the poor, for the abandoned, for the unwanted, for the suffering and for those who have no one to help them. Mary, the *Theotokos*, is always there for them.

From the very moment of our baptism, as we become fully incorporated into the Body of Christ, Mary's presence becomes very real. She is our mother, our friend, our solace, our helper, our refuge in time of danger, and our consolation in time of distress. We look to Mary during periods of darkness to be our luminous guide and our hope in the midst of despair. As we journey towards God's kingdom, Mary's warm presence dispels our feelings of loneliness. She, the *Theotokos*, gives the needed strength and courage to complete the journey. We walk as Christians but never alone, for the Mother of God is always by our side. If we learn to remain quiet, live by Gospel simplicity, and don't fuss too much about ourselves, we should be able to sense her continually consoling presence as we take each step on the road to God's kingdom.

Holy Mother of God,
by the example of your pure simplicity
and your utter humility
you attracted the eyes of the Lord
and touched the depths of his heart.
Inspire us to follow in your footsteps
that we may also please him
all the days of our earthly life.

BROTHER VICTOR-ANTOINE

Simplicity and the Desert Ideal

SAINTS JOHN THE BAPTIST, ANTONY THE GREAT, AND MARY OF EGYPT

The wilderness and the dry land shall be glad,
the desert shall rejoice and blossom...

ISAIAH 35:1

Christian monastic life had its simple, unpretentious, humble origins in the deserts of Egypt and Palestine. Moved by the radical call to live by Gospel simplicity, the first monastics went to the desert in the search for God alone, to pursue there a life of union with him. Those early monastics discovered that the desert was a very unique place, for it was there, following the biblical accounts, that God had revealed himself in all his glory to Moses. During those long forty years in the desert, the Lord in his kindness had fed his people with manna from above. And he also refreshed them with water from a rock. Later on, it was also in that Sinai wilderness that the prophet Elias met God and had that unforgettable dialogue with him.

We read in the New Testament that John the Baptist went into the desert to prepare the way for the Lord. Later on, Christ himself would be led into the desert by the Holy Spirit to prepare himself for the mission for which the Father had sent him. We also read in the Gospels that he returned again and again to the solitude of the desert to rest and pray during those three years of his intense ministry. Shortly before his passion, at a deserted place in Mount Tabor, he lifted for a short time the veil of his humanity and revealed to a few chosen Apostles the splendor of his divinity.

In retiring to the wilderness, the early monastics were not directly seeking to cut themselves off from all human fellowship or contact with others. After all, they knew well the Christian life consists in communion with Christ and all those who form part of his Body. Instead, their objective was to seek God with purity of heart and unhindered simplicity, away from the vanity and worldly cares of society. The times the early Desert Fathers and Mothers inhabited were as turbulent and confusing as our own today, and not just the civil society, but also the ecclesiastical institutions of the Church of God. In the midst of all this noise and confusion, the message and simplicity of the Gospel often became blurred or forgotten, and they wanted to do something to remedy it. Following the example of the Apostles and martyrs, the early desert monks refused to compromise with the world or its values. Instead, they quietly sought refuge apart, in the distant wilderness, where they could clearly hear the Word of God and in all simplicity live by its true teachings. The monastic movement owes its origins to this early desert adventure, an adventure that ever since has shaped and influenced all of monastic life for successive centuries. The call to the solitude, the silence, and the stark simplicity of the desert remains even today a constant element in the monastic vocation.

There is one thing these early monastics in their profound realism could help us learn today, and that is that the desert does not always have to be a geographical place. Most appropriately, it can be found in the solitary innermost place of our own hearts. What really counts is our own attitude of pure simplicity. Prayer has always been the one indispensable activity of life in the monastic desert, and today we can also pray anywhere, in any place. All we need to do is to heed the Gospel's invitation: "But whenever you pray, go into your room and shut the door and pray to your Father who is in secret..." (Matthew 6:6). Unceasing prayer combined with simplicity of life and the daily practice of the basic virtues of charity, humility, obedience, and self-denial: these were the Christian ideals and daily task of those early monastics in their solitary wilderness. These ideals remain valid today, not only for monks and nuns, but also for Christians of all ways of life and persuasion. Ultimately, it means making a serious commitment to follow Christ by taking both the Gospel and our Christian life seriously.

Today, many Christians retire for periods of time to a hermitage in a quiet, isolated place. Some monks and nuns try to re-establish the ideals of the wilderness by once a week or once a month taking a "desert day," depending on their circumstances, in complete solitude and silence. These "hermit days," as they are often called, allow those who plunge into the desert solitude the opportunity to encounter God, the absolute, in his profound mystery. It also provides the occasion for the hermit to confront himself and the crude reality of his own sinfulness. All those who assiduously give themselves to this particular practice attest to its immense help and value for a true spiritual life. This desert experience, rediscovered anew today in all its freshness and simplicity, has become so essential for our ordinary Christian lives that many monasteries hospitably share with their fellow men and women their own spaces of solitude and silence, allowing both Christian and non-Christians alike to partake in the mystery and benefit of desert solitude.

SAINT JOHN THE BAPTIST: *A VOICE CRIES OUT IN THE DESERT*

Each year, during our annual Advent pilgrimage, we frequently encounter in the Scripture and liturgical readings the desert figure of John the Baptist, the forerunner of Christ. During those blessed Advent days, we feel his presence intimately and hear the urgency of his message: "Prepare the way of the Lord, make his paths straight" (Matthew 3:3). We also hear the Master's words: "What then did you go out to see? A prophet? Yes, I tell you, and more than a prophet. This is the one about whom it is written, 'See, I am sending my messenger ahead of you, who will prepare your way before you'" (Matthew 11:9–10). The desert presence of the forerunner provides a powerful incentive during our early preparation days for Christmas, and it remains with us long after. In fact, it is there with us at the feast of the Theophany, the climax of the Christmas season, when we commemorate Jesus' baptism by the Baptist in the river Jordan. This unique occasion is the first moment in the New Testament when the presence of the entire Trinity is revealed!

From all eternity, God chose the desert as the place to mentor and prepare John the Baptist for the role he was to assume in the New Testament. In the desert wasteland, John is taught from above to instigate and herald the good news of the Savior's arrival into this world. He is to go ahead and prepare a way for him. John the Baptist, the humble and simple desert dweller, the hermit who lives on herbs and wild honey, is allotted the unique mission of pointing out Christ the Savior to all others. "Here is the Lamb of God who takes away the sin of the world!" (John 1:29). He is both the Lord's forerunner and the friend of the Bridegroom. From the depths of the desert, in all his stark simplicity, John the Baptist urges us to prepare for the Lord's coming by embracing the way of conversion and humble repentance. It is by embracing the work of personal repentance that we can level out the hills and the valleys in our hearts and thus make a straight path for the Lord. John the Baptist is a model of desert simplicity for all Christians; indeed, for all of us. Though he is sometimes represented as the harsh, fiery figure of the Old Testament prophets, he was particularly dear to Jesus who went as far as to declare: "'...among those born of women no one has arisen greater than John the Baptist'" (Matthew 11:11).

Appropriately, the simple and profound desert personality of John the Baptist fitted perfectly within God's plan for the unfolding of the mystery of the Incarnation. From the earliest moments in his mother's womb, John reveled in his singular association with the Incarnate Son of God. Filled with the Holy Spirit even from his mother's womb, he leaped with joy at the nearness of the Lord Incarnate present in Mary's womb.

John, the desert dweller, was given the unique privilege of being among the first to greet the Savior's arrival in our world, to announce and proclaim his coming, and, lastly, to pour the baptismal waters upon his head as the heavens opened and the mystery of the entire Trinity was revealed for the first time in all its glory!

SAINT ANTONY THE GREAT: *DESERT SIMPLICITY AND THE WORK OF LOVE*

Antony was still a rather young man when he decided to retire to the solitude of the desert to follow Christ. One day while worshipping in church, he heard the Gospel text: ..."'If you wish to be perfect, go, sell your possessions, and give the money to the poor, and you will have treasure in heaven; then come, follow me'" (Matthew 9:21). At that very moment, stricken by a movement of grace, he decided to leave all things behind and retire immediately to the desert wilderness.

In the desert, he learned slowly but steadily to prioritize all his mental, physical, and emotional energies and to place them entirely at the Lord's service in the search for his divine will. He learned in the desert that all that mattered was to center one's life wholly in God and to live in constant union with him. From his early age, Antony experienced an intense attachment to the person of Christ. He made Saint Paul's words his own: "For me, to live is Christ." Consequently, he applied all his mental energies to the continual meditation of the Word of God, especially the holy Gospels. His life in the desert was so Christ-centered that before he died, his last advice to his disciples was: "Always breathe Christ and trust him."

Saint Antony retired to the wilderness solitude with typical Gospel simplicity, without creating any noise or calling any attention to himself. He did not choose the desert as a form of escape, but rather as the unique place where he could learn to put into practice the teachings of the Gospel. From the beginning, he understood that all basic and sincere Christian life is built upon two pillars: the two commandments of love of God and love of neighbor. Daily he strove to live by these two commandments. He knew that his intimate relationship with the Lord was tested by how he interacted with others, by the way he treated each and every human being he encountered, wherever he happened to be. Even in the desert, one couldn't totally avoid all human contacts. Besides, as another Desert Father, Abba Apolle points out, Antony knew there was an intrinsic unity between the commandment to love God and the commandment to love our neighbor: "A person who sees his brother sees his God."

The characteristic simplicity of the desert had an immensely beneficial impact on Saint Antony. There is nothing like the bareness and starkness of the desert to help one see all reality with greater clarity, in the light of the eternity of God. In the empty desolation of the desert, removed from the noise, shadows, and confusion of the society of his days, Saint Anthony embraced fully the work of learning to love, as God himself loves his own creatures. Often in daily life, the only image of God we are allowed to see is that of our neighbor next to us. Be it a friend or a stranger, someone pleasant or disagreeable, that someone is always made in God's own image and is consequently worthy of all our love. Each encounter with another human being, however slight or profound, is a sacrament where we personally meet Christ the Lord. The smallest and most trivial of the actions we perform to aid or hurt any human being—a neighbor—is done directly to Christ himself. With startling simplicity, Jesus reminds us: "Truly I tell you, just as you did it to one of the least of these who are members of my family, you did it to me" (Matthew 25:40). There is an apotegma attributed to Saint Antony that speaks volumes as to how strongly and deeply the desert saint engrossed himself in the work of love, making it his primary concern. Speaking to one of his disciples, Antony said, "Our life and our death is with our neighbor. If we have gained our brother, we have gained God, but if we scandalize our brother, we have sinned against Christ" (Antony the Great, *Apotegma* 9). From his desert solitude, Anthony reminds us that the love of God and the love of neighbor are intimately linked. One is an integral component of the other. For him, as it should be for all of us, the work of love is the principal purpose of all serious Christian spirituality. Though isolated in the desert, Anthony found a way to put into daily practice the admonition of the Apostle John: "Beloved, since God loved us so much, we also ought to love one another. No one has ever seen God; if we love one another, God lives in us, and his love is perfected in us" (1 John 4:11–12).

Wrapped in Gospel simplicity, Saint Antony attained in the desert the Christian ideal: to make the work of love the ultimate rule and purpose of his entire life. Similarly, the work of love, carried out daily in simplicity and humility, is an absolute for all of Jesus' disciples, that is all of us. It is very real and it absorbs us wholly when we discover the reality of God's presence in others. In the end, whether in the silence of a physical desert or the boisterous desert of the crowds, love alone remains...and it is on how much we have loved God and our neighbor that at the end we shall be judged.

SAINT MARY OF EGYPT:
DESERT SIMPLICTY AND THE WORK OF REPENTANCE

Every year, usually during the middle of Lent (April 2nd), we celebrate the memorial of a saint who embodies the very spirit of Lent and the mystery of repentance. Like Christ, our Master, who retired to the Judean desert to make war with the evil one and prepare for the ministry the Father had sent him, so did Saint Mary the Egyptian after having received the extraordinary grace of conversion.

Prior to her journey into the Judean desert, Mary had spent a great amount of her time as a public sinner, a prostitute, corrupting many of the young in her native Egypt. She delighted in earthly pleasures, entertaining those who sought her company, often refusing to take payments for her services. For her, pleasure alone justified her behavior. One day she hastily joined a group of pilgrims making their way from Cairo to the holy city of Jerusalem. These pilgrims were going to Jerusalem with the express intent of celebrating the feast of the Exaltation of the Holy Cross on September 14. Being both anxious and curious about venerating the true cross, she followed the pilgrims on their way to the church where the cross was first discovered. However, every time she tried to enter the church and move forward towards the cross, a mysterious force prevented her from doing so. While all the other pilgrims could easily approach the cross, she was paralyzed. Depressed by her useless attempts to enter the church and venerate the cross, she felt a sense of divine rejection. Still bewildered by the experience, she turned to an icon of the Mother of God and earnestly prayed to the Blessed Virgin Mary, the Holy *Theotokos.* In humility, Saint Mary confessed to her sinful life and begged to be rescued from the degrading life that had enveloped her in shame. Her inner most longing expressed during her prayer in the most intimate of language was for the redemption of the holy cross. In repentance and great love for Christ's salvation, Saint Mary promised to give up the world of sin and live chastely thereafter. As Mary the Egyptian prayed so fervently to the most gracious *Theotokos,* she received the grace to move forward towards Christ's cross. She then continued her journey forwards to the river Jordan, and after traversing its waters, moved further and forward to the destination indicated for her by the Mother of God: the desert. The empty Judean desert was the place chosen by God where Mary would spend her remaining years—more than forty—living out faithfully, daily, this unique encounter between human repentance and God's loving mercy.

Saint Mary of Egypt is a very atypical saint, a saint almost forgotten these days, except maybe by those who embrace a desert type of monastic life. The holiness of Saint Mary of Egypt can perhaps be ascertained at different levels, and some may get tempted to do just that. However, as we immerse ourselves in the short story of her life, there are two aspects that jump before our eyes immediately: the mystery of repentance and the reality of the desert. Saint Mary's life confronts us with these two aspects of the Christian ascesis by actually bringing both into one. In her case, the narrow and hard way of repentance led her to the solitude and seeming spiritual futility of a place of desolation: the desert.

Saint Mary understood well the depths of the Gospel words: "For the gate is narrow and the road is hard that leads to life" (Matthew 7:13–14). The Gospel, the "Good News," is refreshing because when we accept it with faith and true simplicity, as did Saint Mary, we become cognizant of a new life in contrast to the old one we knew. The previous life was one subject to sin, to passions, to corruption, to evil, and ultimately to the death of the spirit. In spite of its many allures, anyone who has tasted even partially a life of earthly pleasures knows deep within him or herself that it is nothing but pure emptiness and deception. The new life offered by Christ, on the contrary, contains the promise of eternal life, a life of intimacy with the God of all joy and peace.

The Gospels are firm on the fact that for Christians to attain this new life in Christ, we must first renounce the old one of sin and corruption and embrace a life of repentance and discipleship. Through the mystery and grace attached to repentance, we crucify and bury our old self in the very cross of Christ. From then on, we find our true freedom in carrying Christ's cross and being buried in his tomb. The mystery of repentance is encapsulated in the stark reality of Good Friday and Holy Saturday. Without it, we could never arrive to the experience of new life in Christ, and to the taste of his victorious resurrection.

Saint Mary went further than repentance. She confronted and accepted the fact that she needed a suitable place, the desert, to live out daily her call to repentance. Clothed with the power of love, constant prayer, and the tears of repentance, Saint Mary made the desert fertile with the fruits of her humble holiness. Rejected by those who knew her before, she nevertheless prayed to the Mother of God for guidance with deep humility and simplicity. And the Most Holy *Theotokos*, the Mother of all those who embrace a sincere life of repentance, never failed her. She showed Saint Mary of Egypt the path to the most interior spots in the desert. The Mother of God, whose intercession was the supreme instrument in Saint Mary's conversion, was intimately involved in preparing a place where Saint Mary could spend every minute of her entire life with Christ, her divine Savior. The *Theotokos*, Saint Mary of Egypt's faithful protector and companion, encouraged and sustained her, as Mary the Egyptian moved forward from the veneration of the true cross in Jerusalem to the unmistakable reality of the desert beyond the Jordan.

Now totally alone, with Christ and his mother as her sole companions, Saint Mary would spend her desert years immersed in the simplicity of the one task: the work of love and continual repentance. Because of her absolute love for Christ, her Savior, she would endure the desert's burning heat during the day and its freezing cold nights. She would also endure endless temptation and the longings of the flesh, would be assailed by despair and fear, and yet, aided by the *Theotokos*, she would succumb to none. In the living presence of Christ, her God and Redeemer, and in the arms of the *Theotokos*, her mother and protector, Mary of Egypt found the necessary strength that ultimately led her to the peace and consolation that God alone can give.

In meditating throughout the years on the life and holiness of Saint Mary of Egypt, one can't help but see the relevance of the desert in her spiritual development. It is precisely the monotony and the stark simplicity of the desert that led to the blossoming and depth of repentance in her heart, which in turn explains her unusual path to holiness. The distinctiveness of a place is always important in one's spiritual life. One must bloom where one is planted, as the old adage says. This is evident throughout the Bible, where we see the Lord choose certain sites for specific actions as part of his revelation. For instance, we see in the Old Testament the relevance of Mount Sinai for the revelation of the Law. In the New Testament, every action of Christ is tied to a specific place: Bethlehem, Nazareth, Jordan, Cana, Mount Tabor, Mount of Olives, Jerusalem, Calvary, the sea of Galilee, and so on. We also discover that the desert, as a place, plays a unique role both in the Old and the New Testament. The desert, the place where the Lord goes to do battle with the demons, is also the place sanctified and made holy by his presence.

Centuries later, successions of Christians, monks and nuns would follow in the Lord's footsteps and withdraw to the desert wilderness, either to that of Egypt or Judea as Mary the Egyptian did, or to any other, for the sake of embracing the hard and narrow way of the Gospel. The continual asceticism of these fervent desert Christians was expressed through their constant vigils of fasting, reading, silence, obedience, constant prayer, manual labor, charity, and hospitality. The harsh reality of the desert was embraced by them for one sole purpose: repentance and unceasing union with God.

Divine Master,
you loved the barren simplicity,
the silence and solitude of the desert.
You often retired to it to pray
and made it your home for forty days.
May we learn to listen to your voice
in that unique desert solitude: the depths of our own hearts.

BROTHER VICTOR-ANTOINE

Simplicity and a Christ-centered Life

SAINT BENEDICT

With the Gospel for our guide, may we deserve to see him who has called us to his kingdom.

PROLOGUE OF THE RULE

From the moment one opens Saint Benedict's Rule, we observe that every page is imbued with the presence of the authentic Christ from the Gospels. From opening prologue, Saint Benedict leads the disciple directly to the source and reason for the Rule. He gently summons the disciple to incline the ears of his heart, to listen attentively, to undertake the noble weapon of obedience in order to do battle for the true King, Christ the Lord. He presents the disciple with the mystery of the person of Christ who alone is the source of our living faith and who alone can provide true nourishment for our inner life.

For Saint Benedict, Christ is the starting point, the in-between, and the end point towards whom he directs the disciple. The unfolding of the rest of the Rule has no other purpose but to lead the disciple to encounter this Christ of the Gospels, this living Christ, this Christ who, though abiding in his ever-transcendent mystery, offers himself to us in the simplicity and humility of his humanity. The Book of the Gospels, which Saint Benedict offers as a guide to the disciple, contains the mystery of the Word. It is by faithfully listening with the heart's ears to every utterance from the Word, and learning to live by it, that the disciple can slowly begin to discover and enter into the mystery of him who is the Way, the Truth, and the Life. As Raymond Brown used to remind us in his lectures at

Union Theological Seminary (which I had the privilege to attend from to time to time), Christ is the way because he teaches the truth, and this leads to the true life.

After the Prologue, as we go on reading and meditating on each sentence from the Rule, we arrive to the fourth chapter, and there we find a sentence that seems to summarize the entire Rule. Straightforward and with moving simplicity, Saint Benedict emphatically counsels the disciple to "prefer nothing to the love of Christ." For Saint Benedict, our entire human-Christian existence, the entire monastic ethos, exists only to point to Christ, the Alpha and the Omega. Christ is the focal point of the monk's life. All things in time and in daily life are ordered to achieve this end: the persevering of the disciple in the intense activity of loving his Master, Christ the Lord. For Saint Benedict, the love of Christ is the beginning and the end of the monastic life, its only goal and purpose. In learning to love Christ above all else, the disciple ascertains from Saint Benedict that all things are possible to achieve in his otherwise humble and simple monastic life. He also learns the contrary: that without Christ his life, monastic life itself offers no sense.

The monastic life traces its origins to the Gospels. From the Scriptures we learn that Christ invites some disciples to leave all possessions aside in order to follow him. The disciple is urged by the Lord to renounce not only possessions, but also marriage and a normal family life, the freedom to move and do as he or she pleases, and his or her own will—to forsake all for the imitation of Christ's own life on earth and the kingdom of heaven. To accept to follow Christ, to imitate his life on earth, implies embracing the simplicity of the Gospels in its totality. This Gospel simplicity is a form of dedicated love, an outcome of love of the disciple for the Master, a creative expression and imitation of him who emptied himself to assume our humanity out of love for each of us. Through the embracing of this Gospel simplicity with love, Saint Benedict teaches the disciple to penetrate the very life of God himself, which is divine love. For God is love, and Jesus Christ his Son, the ultimate manifestation of this love.

For Saint Benedict, Christ is the center and only reason for the monk's life. This means that all activities, realities, and whatever else the monk' s life is engaged with acquire their *raison d'etre* from the monk's personal and passionate attachment to the person of Christ. Saint Benedict envisions the daily monastic journey—the monastic day itself from Vigils to Compline—as the means of which to provide a continual and personal access to Christ. The daily liturgy and its offices, the *lectio divina*, the times of silent prayer, the daily manual or intellectual work, the meetings among the brethren and the guests, the interchanges with the abbot who takes the place of Christ in the monastery, are all real occasions for the monastic to personally encounter Christ in all the particulars of daily life. As a wise master of the spiritual life, Saint Benedict designed the monastic daily to be such, so that its every moment and circumstance will give the monk or nun the occasion to come close to Christ, to touch him and to be touched by him.

Through every particle of the Rule, Saint Benedict wishes to transmit to the disciple his own living attachment to the person of Christ and help make this attachment the disciple's own. He often cites Saint Paul throughout the Rule, and this should not come as a surprise to anyone. The Christo-centric character of the letters of Saint Paul conveyed an appeal for Saint Benedict equal to none, except for the Gospels—the words of the Lord himself. Saint Benedict certainly made Paul's words his own: "For me, to live is Christ." For the humble Benedict, the only thing that truly mattered was that at all times and in all occasions he found himself to be "in Christ." This continual communion with Christ was the aim and goal he proposed to all his disciples.

If there is any purpose to the Benedictine Rule, it is that of teaching and leading the disciple to this life in Christ, to this intimate communion with our Lord and Savior. Through Christ, and through him alone, the Christian is introduced to communion with the Father. It is Christ alone who opens wide the doors of the mystery and reveals to us the Father's tender love for each one of us, his creatures. This would have never been possible without Christ. Jesus is the way to the Father. He is the image of the Father and he is the only one who can fully reconcile us and give us access to the Father. To the extent that we experience intimately in our hearts the presence of Christ, we experience also that of his loving Father, the Father of us all and the origin of all things.

The love and knowledge of Jesus Christ experienced in the depths of our hearts inexorably leads us to the experience and knowledge of the Father's love for all and each of us. There lies the great mystery. Christ is for us the way to the Father, and he introduces us to that intimate communion of love which he shares with the Father and the Holy Spirit. To be found "in Christ," to abide in him permanently, therefore, means to share in this intimate relationship with the three divine Persons. Saint Benedict impregnates the disciple with the certainty that in Christ all things are brought together, that through him alone the ultimate realities of God's saving actions are rendered present to the whole world. The summit of all mystical life, according to Saint Simeon the New Theologian, is precisely this personal encounter with Christ, who in turn shows us the Father and continues to speak in our hearts through the Holy Spirit.

The many long years of living under the Rule, of trying to digest Saint Benedict's thoughts and absorb his teachings, have shown me that basically there is a strong pedagogy to the Rule, a basic unity based on the unique intuition of Saint Benedict himself. From the beginning of the Rule to the very last chapter, Saint Benedict gradually and with utter simplicity and insight introduces the disciple to the discovery of true Gospel living. Chapter after chapter in the Rule unfold the many and distinct aspects that characterize a true evangelical life. The Lord himself teaches us that the disciple is not greater than the master; therefore Benedict approaches the monastic life as the disciple's path to follow and imitate his Master, Christ the Lord.

Essentially for Saint Benedict, a true monastic life consists in the *imitatio Christi*, the faithful imitation and following of the life-example and teachings from the Master, hence Saint Benedict's directives to the disciple to learn to walk in the steps of the Gospel. With true simplicity and wisdom, Saint Benedict unfolds in each chapter of the Rule the disciple's humble and unique way of treading in Christ's footsteps, of each day growing in deeper friendship with him. The Gospel and the person of Christ are inseparable. The Gospel is the Book of Life. It is there, and there alone, that we find the Truth and the Light. The Christ of Bethlehem and the Christ of the cross, the Christ of the Eucharist and the Christ of the resurrection are at all times present in the Gospel. In the mystery of the Gospel we discover Christ present in his childhood years; Christ in his hidden life in Nazareth with Mary and Joseph; Christ teaching in the Temple in Jerusalem; Christ gathering his disciples; Christ preaching throughout Judea and Jerusalem; Christ praying long nights in the desert solitude; Christ healing the sick and nourishing the multitude; Christ, the friend of Mary, Martha, and

Lazarus; Christ proclaiming the Beatitudes; Christ undergoing his passion and resurrecting on the third day; Christ ascending to his Father while promising to send us the Comforter.

When the Gospel is proclaimed during our daily offices and worship, we are captured, so to speak, by Christ's mysterious presence. At the hearing of the Gospel, we are there with Christ as he is with the Father. The events in the Gospel may at times seem very remote, yet they are also so near and close at hand. The events of the past and the present time somehow converge in the actual presence of Christ, in the "today" of God, as the Gospels are read, meditated, absorbed, and put into practice. Jesus is present in the mystery of the Word today, just as much as he was when the events took place in history. When Saint Benedict counsels the disciple to "walk in the ways of the Gospel," he is inviting him to enter into this profound reality, the mystery of Christ ever-present in his Word. The Christian journey, the monastic journey, consists precisely in this daily discovery of Christ the *Logos*, the Word, as present in the Gospels. There, we discover him and we touch the hem of his garments; we listen to his voice while quietly absorbing his teachings; we learn to eat of his body and drink of his blood while being assimilated by him in the Eucharist. What is more, in the process of this assimilation by him we are transformed into him.

When Saint Benedict decided to "establish a school for the Lord's service," he had in mind a certain pedagogy, a particular way of learning and guiding the disciple. In this specific school, according to the method set out by Benedict, the disciple's entire life was exclusively directed to acquiring the knowledge of Jesus Christ and constantly growing in it. Each chapter of the Rule, as the disciple discovers daily, is permeated with the person of Christ, with his teachings, with his life-example as the only model for us to follow. There is no confusion in the Rule for he who in all simplicity aims only to please Christ and live day and night in his company. After all, this intimate friendship with Christ is what sustains every moment of the disciple's daily life. It is there that he gradually learns, as Benedict points out, "to share through patience in the sufferings of Christ" so that one day he may deserve to share in the joys of his kingdom. In this school, the disciple learns from Saint Benedict to let go of his own plans and expectations as to seek only the path of Christ's commandments and the inexpressible delight of his love. As Thomas Merton beautifully expresses, "The monastic life is life in the Spirit of Christ, a life in which the Christian gives himself entirely to the love of God which transforms him in the light of Christ." All else is rubbish and of no consequence to the disciple.

There is a timeless appeal in Saint Benedict's particular approach to persuing a Christ-centered life. Some may think that this Christ-centered life as proposed by Saint Benedict in his Rule can only apply to those who embrace the monastic life, that is, monastics. I think Saint Benedict would be the first to disagree with that perception. Saint Benedict, who once had a vision of a luminous globe like the sun containing everything and everyone in it in God, never envisioned a special cast of people as followers of Christ, and neither did the Desert Fathers and Mothers.

The monks at the time of the Desert Fathers and of Saint Benedict himself were simple lay Christians who wanted to follow the radical path of the Gospel without any encumbrances. This desire to follow Christ closely led them to the solitude of the wilderness, or in the case of Saint Benedict, to the solitude of Subiaco. They never intended to found a so-called "religious or monastic order." When lay disciples gathered around him and asked him to be their leader,

Saint Benedict made recourse to a Rule as a unifying principle. Because the Rule was so simple, sober, and balanced in all aspects, it went on to become what it is today: a way of intensely living one's Christian life, a Gospel way of following Christ. Saint Benedict never ceased to emphasize that the only purpose of all Christian life, monastic or otherwise, was for the disciple to be found at all times "in Christ." As Saint Paul assured us, to be found in Christ is to be a new creation (see 2 Corinthians 5:17). For the disciple as for Saint Benedict, this meant to be absorbed in Christ, to think and to act like him. Furthermore, it meant to live in a perpetual and loving relationship of intimate friendship with Christ.

Throughout the centuries, and especially in our times, new ways of following Christ have surfaced in the Christian church. New Christian movements and even new religious orders have emerged. Interestingly, they each seem to emphasize one particular aspect of the Gospel message, or a particular aspect of Christian spirituality. In retrospect, this would have been incomprehensible to Saint Benedict or to the early desert monks and nuns. This is incomprehensible to Eastern Christians as well, or to those who follow the monastic life in the tradition of the early Eastern churches. For the Eastern monks as for Saint Benedict, it is not a question of embracing or emphasizing one particular aspect of Christian spirituality. For them, there was only one spirituality and one way of living, that of the entire Gospels. For Saint Benedict, the only thing that counted was to be found "in Christ." Christ was the beginning and the end, and nowhere in the early Christian tradition was there a necessity for emphasizing one aspect of a Christ-centered life over other ways of following the Lord. Certainly, this tendency was developed in the Christian West and became overemphasized after the separation of the Eastern and Western churches in 1054. To think and act otherwise would have been anathema for the early Christians, and equally so for the early monastics. Today we live with this ambivalence, this duality with endless interpretations, variations, and ramifications of the Gospel message, when in fact it is all one, as it was for Saint Benedict and all those who preceded him.

Therein lies the wisdom of Saint Benedict, presented to us today as it was to the people of his times: the unity of the mystery of Christ as revealed in the Gospels—a unity that is above all realized in the intimate relationship of the disciple with his Master, Christ the Lord. There is nothing sweeter to the disciple, according to the intuition of Saint Benedict, than to undertake the Lord's yoke and the pure constraints of the Gospel. By accepting to live thus, daily, in all purity, humility, charity, and Gospel simplicity, the disciple can't help but have a small impact upon his surrounding world. His is the privilege of exuding "the sweet odor of Christ" to all those who approach him or come close to him.

Dear Lord,
We praise you for the holy life of Saint Benedict.
His one concern was to follow Christ
and please God alone.
May we follow the wisdom path of his teachings
by preferring Christ above all things,
and by choosing the Gospel as our sole guide.

BROTHER VICTOR-ANTOINE

Simplicity and the Mystery of Suffering

SAINT BERNADETTE

And not only that, but we also boast in our sufferings, knowing that suffering produces endurance, and endurance produces character, and character produces hope, and hope does not disappoint us, because God's love has been poured into our hearts through the Holy Spirit that has been given to us.

ROMANS 5:3–5

I profess a profound attachment to Lourdes and Saint Bernadette for many personal reasons. Naturally, then, I have chosen her in particular as a superb exemplar of both Gospel simplicity and willful acceptance of the mystery of suffering in this life, all in imitation and for the sake of Christ. There is no doubt among Saint Bernadette experts and historians that the young girl from Lourdes captivated those who knew her, in part because of her extraordinary simplicity of soul. In many ways, this charming peasant-like simplicity seemed to come naturally to Bernadette. This should not come as a surprise to anyone, for as the old theological axiom expresses so well, "grace builds on nature."

The humble Pyrenees peasants, especially the mountain shepherds with their herds, are well known for their exquisite and child-like simplicity. I am particularly cognizant of this every time I return to my roots in those cherished mountains and its native people. Today, they still speak the *patois* from the time of Bernadette, and more importantly, they still behave with that straightforward simplicity from times past, which is becoming more and more elusive everywhere else.

To be frank about Bernadette's simplicity, we must acknowledge that it was not all just based on her cultural upbringing. Besides the obvious simplicity springing from her origin and background, there is also the simplicity of life that Bernadette wholeheartedly embraced in order to follow Jesus, her Master. Saint Bernadette attended Mass regularly, where she heard the Gospel stories and teachings that propelled her to become a faithful disciple of her Master. As she learned to read and digest her weekly catechism lessons, she became more and more enamored of the Christ of the Gospels. In reading and meditating on the Gospels, Saint Bernadette found Jesus her Savior, the Good Shepherd. She found the truth, and more precisely, she found the living example of him whom she was called to imitate.

As a young girl she heard the invitation: "Learn from me, for I am meek and humble of heart" whispered by the Master in her heart. To this she responded and assented with her entire being, involving all her behavior, mind, body, and soul. The Lord bestowed upon Bernadette the grace of this extraordinary simplicity, one that would serve her well all the days of her life. This particular grace prepared her most suitably for the events that later were to change her life forever.

Bernadette Soubirous was born on a freezing cold day in the Pyrenees in January 1844. She was the eldest of four children, and often they did not have enough bread or other food to nourish them daily. When she was eleven years old, she contracted cholera, a prevalent disease at that time, and though she eventually was able to recover, she was left with a permanent asthmatic condition and poor health for her remaining years. The family inhabited a damp, uncomfortable room named Le Cachot, which pilgrims today can still visit in the center of the town of Lourdes. Bernadette's father was a local miller, and unfortunately he was often without a job to support the family. To help the family survive, Bernadette was sent to the home of Marie Lagues, her former wet-nurse, in a nearby village named Bartres.

In Bartres, Bernadette was employed as a shepherdess, minding with typical peasant simplicity a small flock of sheep. While at Bartres, Bernadette began attending catechism lessons in the parish, thus receiving a solid foundation of her Christian faith. She loved her stay on the local Bartres farm. The many silent hours she spent outdoors in the fields pasturing her flock were used particularly to apply herself to prayer and the recitation of the rosary. She managed to spend the summer months at Bartres, but in the winter she always returned home to help her parents with the care of her siblings.

In spite of the dire poverty at Le Cachot, Bernadette was happy to be home. She loved intensely and with great simplicity both her parents and her siblings. As a typical child from the Pyrenees, she was affectionate, friendly, and always ready to help those most in need, especially her own family. When available, she often accepted small tasks around Lourdes so that she could help her parents and the rest of the family. As with most poor families in the locality, food was often scarce at the Soubious home, and Bernadette wished to contribute to the family table in whatever way possible.

From a very early age, Bernadette developed a deep trust in God and an undivided confidence in the Mother of God. She often prayed asking Our Lady's consoling protection in all her daily undertakings. Every night, she recited the rosary and participated in other prayer devotions with her family. On Sunday they all attended Mass at the local church. The family neighbors all knew that the young shepherdess, Bernadette, was a pious and devout girl, someone who never forgot to carry her rosary in her pocket. Bernadette's simple and profound faith was based on the basic recognition and deep meaning of her baptismal grace. She knew that through baptism she had become a child of God and was thus deeply loved by him.

An extraordinary adventure began for this simple Pyrenees peasant on February 11, 1858. While accompanying her sister, Toinette, and neighbor, Jeanne, in search of wood for the fire near the grotto of Massabielle, a beautiful young lady dressed in white suddenly appeared to Bernadette from deep within the Massabielle cave. These extraordinary visions continued for several months, until the final one on July 16, the feast of Our Lady of Mount Carmel. On the day of that final apparition, the beautiful lady in white revealed her name to Bernadette in the Bigourdan dialect of the Pyrenees, saying: "Que soy era Immaculada Conceptiou," which literally means, "I am the Immaculate Conception."

From then on, thousands of people converged to Lourdes interested in meeting the humble peasant shepherdess. They all took an extraordinary interest in her. They all tried to examine and scrutinize her life, her story, her behavior, her judgments. Many accused her of being mad, and Bernadette had to face hostility from both the civil and Church authorities. Public opinion and the media, always in search of vain sensationalism, were not always kind to this rather simple peasant girl.

Bernadette, with rare discretion and utmost simplicity, tried to avoid all this endless curiosity and reinforced instead her own spiritual priorities. With deep gratitude for the graces received, she continued her life of prayer and intimacy with God and Our Lady. She did this daily, with humility and her characteristic simplicity. Both simplicity and humility were her favorite virtues. They came naturally to someone like her, who was raised in typical fashion. She meditated daily on Our Lady's message, an invitation to all to constant prayer and inner conversion in the true spirit of the Gospel. The curiosity and indiscretion from visitors never stopped; it continued to invade the little privacy she enjoyed.

Bernadette loved Lourdes, the grotto, and her family and friends, and was not eager to depart from there. On the other hand, she longed to disappear from the raving crowds and aspired to a quiet religious life of continual communion with God. She was close to the Sisters of Charity of Nevers, whom she deeply admired, especially in their dedication to the poor. She asked to be admitted to their novitiate. Reluctantly, and with great sadness, Bernadette left Lourdes and all it entailed: the grotto, her family, her Pyrenees mountains, and the successive sheep flocks, and made the long journey to Nevers by train. There she received the name of Sister Marie-Bernard and made her religious profession on October 30, 1867.

In the Nevers convent, Bernadette encountered again and again the mystery of suffering. She suffered both physically and internally. She was of fragile health and thus constantly sick. She also endured much incomprehension and despondency from the part of those she lived with, her own sisters in religious life. When people came to the Nevers convent asking for her, they were often told in her presence that "she was good for nothing." Filled with her usual humility and simplicity, she faced her daily pain, repeating to herself, "I shall follow the example of Jesus, my Master. I shall carry the cross assigned to me with courage and generosity." Bernadette never tried to escape either the daily humiliations bestowed upon her or the physical suffering sent to her by the Lord. With child-like simplicity, she constantly made recourse to her one true source of support and daily encouragement: prayer. At times, when the pain was unbearable, she would not ask to be relieved from it, but instead uttered frequently to Our Lady: "*O ma Mere, prenez mon coeur et enfoncez-le dans le coeur de mon Jesus*" ("O my Mother, take my heart and hide it in the heart of Jesus").

With true simplicity of heart, Bernadette never responded to suffering by giving in to depression or introspection. She never analyzed her pain or spoke much about it to others. She would simply make recourse to prayer in such instances repeating often: "*O mon Dieu, je vous aime par-dessus toutes choses*" ("O my God, I love you above all things"). Like all true mystics, Bernadette simply refused to dwell on herself, to think about herself, or to give in to the temptation of self-aggrandizement or self-pity.

The temptation to think of oneself as important is so prevalent in the Church of our times. How many Christians today, clergy and non-clergy alike, sometimes including bishops and others in position of power, think of themselves as indispensable, as God's gift to the Church and to the world? It is so sad to witness such a deviation from the truth imparted by the Gospel, from the very example of Christ and his Holy Mother.

Bernadette, acting contrary to all this, made sure that her spiritual itinerary was one of Gospel simplicity and humility. Simplicity was her supreme rule in all things: in her words, her attitudes, her concepts, her behavior, her relationships, her faith, her lifestyle, her prayer, and her approach to suffering. Through simplicity and prayer, she received the grace to endure her daily pains and entered thus into the mysterious sharing of Christ's passion. Saint Bernadette was indeed fascinated by the mysterious symbolism of the cross and its role in our lives. She often insisted in marking places, objects, and the foreheads of those who approached with the sign of the Cross. In the intangible realism of the cross, she saw the mystery of God's love truly at work. The cross symbolized for her the constant memory of Christ's passion, the sign of our salvation, the bulwark and foundation of our faith. The Mother of God told her that she would be happy, not in this world, but in the next. Bernadette found strength and consolation in Our Lady's promise to her, and aimed only at reaching the perfection of charity in this life. Charity, love for one another, was Jesus' last testament to his disciples. And for Bernadette, Jesus was the one Master. She lived only to imitate and please him.

When the end came, on April 16, 1879, during an agony of deep suffering and distress, Bernedette found a last fraction of strength in the crucifix she grasped and placed over her heart. When one of the sisters assisting her asked her if she was suffering much, Bernadette responded with her habitual simplicity: "*Tout cela est bon pour le Ciel*" ("All of it is good to get to heaven"). At three o'clock that afternoon, she who was favored during her life to behold the beauty of the Mother of God, died with the same simplicity she embraced all throughout her earthly journey, after repeating twice: "*Sainte Marie, Mere de Dieu, priez pour moi pauvre pecheuresse*" ("Holy Mary, Mother of God, pray for me a poor sinner"). Consequently, Bernadette, the humble shepherdess who had previously welcomed the visit of the Mother of God with delight and child-like simplicity, passed that afternoon from the mystery of suffering into the eternal joy that God had prepared for her.

Saint Bernadette, Our Lady's little shepherdess, teach us to live in true Gospel simplicity and wisdom, following always God's mysterious ways for each of us!

BROTHER VICTOR-ANTOINE

Simplicity and the Work of Grace

SAINT THÉRÈSE OF LISIEUX

Everything is Grace.

THÉRÉSE OF LISIEUX

Uncreated grace is such a fathomless mystery. It is God's life in us in a manner well beyond our human understanding. Deep down, through a faith that gives light to our inner vision, we know that everything in us is the work of grace, a free gift of grace. Saint Thérèse of Lisieux used to love to repeat, "*Tout est grace*" ("All is grace"). And how right she was! She also loved simplicity and embraced the Gospel teaching of a simple spiritual childhood as her chosen path to God. The whole adventure of her spiritual life is marked by this childhood simplicity, the type of simplicity that led her to a complete abandonment of the power of God's grace in her. She lived a short life—only twenty-four years on earth—but twenty-four years of complete surrender to that grace that led her unceasingly toward God, her heavenly Father, whom she loved above all else with tender and childhood simplicity. There are so many lessons like this that we can learn daily from the saints.

There is an anecdote in Saint Thérèse's life not mentioned often. She loved carrying over her heart a small book of the Gospels. This in itself may seem insignificant and may be considered by some a wholly pious act, an act of devotion. For Saint Thérèse, however, it was an action of capital importance. For her, the book of the Gospels represented the person of Christ, for every utterance contained in the Gospels was the words of Jesus himself. She refused to make distinctions between the person of the Lord and his divine teachings. To her they were one and the same. Jesus, her Master, the "spoken Word from the Father," was one and the same Person in both cases.

Thus, the reverence shown by Thérèse and the saints of old for the book of the Gospels was the same as the reverence shown to the person of Jesus. Saint Thérèse, in her profound faith and utter simplicity, knew that by carrying the book of the Gospels on herself, she was indeed carrying the person of Christ in her heart. This carrying of the Gospels was symbolic of something deeper and a thousand times more important, for by acknowledging the presence of Christ in his words, she was committing herself to the keeping of those very words, to living daily by them.

To someone who once inquired from her about this practice, she replied, "I hear Jesus' words in a new way because they are addressed directly to me." The spirituality of Saint Thérèse was deeply marked by this immersion of herself in the holy Gospels, in the very person of Jesus, the fountain of all grace. Like Our Lady, she knew and carried the Word of God within, and she kept it with humble simplicity and great integrity. She knew Jesus to be the Son of the living God and the source and giver of all grace. She made her own the words of Saint Paul: "Let us therefore approach the throne of grace with boldness, so that we may receive mercy and find grace to help in time of need" (Hebrews 4:16).

Thérèse learned this child-like, genuine simplicity straight from the Gospel. She embraced it wholeheartedly, allowing it to ripen in her a certain sensibility towards the action of grace in her life. The personal action of God in our lives is at times subtle and delicate; it demands perceptiveness on our part, the type of keen awareness children sometimes possess. Saint Thérèse was particularly attracted to those Gospel verses in which Jesus exalts the virtues of children. Those verses spoke to her heart. From them she learned the ways of simplicity Christ expected her to follow, as he did for all his disciples: "Then he took a little child and put it among them; and taking it in his arms, he said to them, 'Whoever welcomes one such child in my name welcomes me, and whoever welcomes me welcomes not me but the one who sent me'" (Mark 9:36–37). If Jesus shows a certain preference for children and portrays them as examples for us to follow, it is because in their simplicity, children are without guile. They don't attribute any favors to themselves and are always ready to acknowledge that everything good comes from God alone.

Saint Thérèse took to heart this lesson from the Gospel. She intuitively knew that if she remained a simple little child in God's arms, it would be the surest way to please him. She read and re-read the verses in the Gospel of Mark and found great consolation in them: "'Let the little children come to me; do not stop them; for it is to such as these that the kingdom of God belongs. Truly I tell you, whoever does not receive the kingdom of God as a little child will never enter it.' And he took them up in his arms, laid his hands on them, and blessed them" (Mark 10:14–16).

By following the example of Saint Thérèse of Lisieux, especially the good examples of simplicity contained in her "little way," we too can arrive at the experiential knowledge that everything is grace, and thus God is at work in us, freely bestowing his grace in our lives. To live by his grace is an invitation to live in deeper communion with him, consenting and acknowledging humbly that all is grace, a free gift from above. We have done nothing to deserve it, and "little ones" that we are, we thank our heavenly Father for all the treasures he bestows on us daily through Jesus, his Son. Union with God is a gift of grace, the ultimate gift, the one that allows us to live in the presence of the living God in an atmosphere of pure simplicity, of inner strength, of deep calm and joy, and childlike trust.

During our moments of silent prayer, we stand before God with the child's attitude of simplicity. We recognize that this very attitude is the action of uncreated grace in us, a pure gift. If at times we find ourselves traversing a period of doubt and inner darkness, we must embrace these inner trials with a certain poverty of spirit, with a simplicity and trust that makes us aware that even these uncertainties are gifts from God. Like Saint Thérèse, who found profound joy in the midst of many trials, we too can experience a deep joy in the act of complete abandonment and submission to the will of the Father. By this simple act of complete surrender to God, of complete trust in his loving providence, we achieve inner freedom from all else that is not God in our lives. In this act of total surrender, in this lucid and complete abandonment into his hands, we find our true peace. Henceforth, we offer and allow God to dispose of us as he pleases. With true simplicity of spirit, with confidence and gratitude to God for his graces, we accept the simple reality that to live by the gifts of God we must first leave the free choice of those gifts to him alone.

Leaning with nothing to lean on
Without light and in darkness
I go burning with Love.
Of love, I have had experience,
Of the good, of the bad that it finds in me
It knows how to benefit (what power)
It changes my soul into itself.

SAINT THÉRÈSE

Acknowledgments

Excerpts by Meister Eckhart from Robert Bernard Blakney, *Meister Eckhart: A Modern Translation* (New York: Harper & Brothers, 1941). Copyright © 1941 Harper & Brothers, copyright renewed. Rights contact: HarperCollins Publishers, Inc. All rights reserved.

Excerpt by Mechthilde of Magdeburg from Mary Caswell Walsh, *Prayers Out of the Depths* (Chicago: Liturgy Training Publications, 2007). All rights reserved.

Excerpts from Thomas Merton, *The Silent Life* (New York: Noonday/ Farrar, Straus and Giroux, 17th printing 1996), copyright © 1957 The Abbey of Our Lady of Gethsemani. All rights reserved; *Thoughts in Solitude* (New York: Farrar, Straus and Giroux, 1999), copyright © 1956, 1958 by The Abbey of Our Lady of Gethsemani. All rights reserved.

Excerpts from Archimandrite Sophrony, *On Prayer*, trans. R. Edmonds (Crestwood, NY: St. Vladimir's Seminary Press, 1998), p. 12. Copyright © 1996 Patriarchal Stavropegic Monastery of St. John the Baptist, Tolleshunt Knights by Maldon, Essex, UK. All rights reserved.

Brother Victor-Antoine

is a resident monk at Our Lady of the Resurrection Monastery, which lives under the Rule of Saint Benedict and is located in upstate New York. He is the author of several books published by Liguori Publications, including the best-selling *Twelve Months of Monastery Soups*, *From a Monastery Kitchen*, and *Sacred Feasts: From a Monastery Kitchen*.

CPSIA information can be obtained
at www.ICGtesting.com
Printed in the USA
BVHW030939290919
559429BV00004B/20/P